UNDERSTANDING PANNENBERG

CASCADE COMPANIONS

The Christian theological tradition provides an embarrassment of riches: from Scripture to modern scholarship, we are blessed with a vast and complex theological inheritance. And yet this feast of traditional riches is too frequently inaccessible to the general reader.

The Cascade Companions series addresses the challenge by publishing books that combine academic rigor with broad appeal and readability. They aim to introduce nonspecialist readers to that vital storehouse of authors, documents, themes, histories, arguments, and movements that comprise this heritage with brief yet compelling volumes.

RECENT TITLES IN THIS SERIES:

UNDERSTANDING PANNENBERG

Landmark Theologian of the Twentieth Century

ANTHONY C. THISELTON

CASCADE *Books* • Eugene, Oregon

UNDERSTANDING PANNENBERG
Landmark Theologian of the Twentieth Century

Cascade Companions

Cascade Books
An Imprint of Wipf and Stock Publishers
199 W. 8th Ave., Suite 3
Eugene, OR 97401

www.wipfandstock.com

PAPERBACK ISBN: 978-1-5326-4125-1
HARDCOVER ISBN: 978-1-5326-4126-8
EBOOK ISBN: 978-1-5326-4127-5

Cataloguing-in-Publication data:

Names: Thiselton, Anthony C., author.

Title: Understanding Pannenberg : landmark theologian of the twentieth century / Anthony C. Thiselton.

Description: Eugene, OR: Cascade Books, 2018 | Series: Cascade Companions | Includes bibliographical references and index.

Identifiers: ISBN 978-1-5326-4125-1 (paperback) | ISBN 978-1-5326-4126-8 (hardcover) | ISBN 978-1-5326-4127-5 (ebook)

Subjects: LCSH: Pannenberg, Wolfhart, 1928–2014—Criticism and interpretation | God (Christianity) | Trinity | Theological anthropology | Jesus Christ—Person and offices | Holy Spirit | Eschatology

Classification: BX4827.P3 T46 2018 (print) | BX4827.P3 (ebook)

Manufactured in the U.S.A.   05/30/18

CONTENTS

PREFACE

I REMAIN ENTRANCED BY the extensive scope, deep learn-
ing, and undoubted incisiveness of Wolfhart Pannenberg's
theology. It constitutes a creative game-changer at the close
of the twentieth century. The days of Bultmann, his school
of existential interpretation, Liberalism, and what he has
called "anthropocentric biblical criticism," are well past. We
look now to new, expanding, horizons.

Even a casual glance at my index of subjects and main
subjects, below, shows that Pannenberg's dominant concerns extend to apocalyptic, church, contingency, creation,
election and predestination, eternity, faith, hermeneutics,
history, resurrection, sin and alienation, the Trinity, truth,
and most especially God, Jesus Christ, and the Holy Spirit.
These cover some sixteen main areas, in addition to more
detailed subjects.

Clearly Pannenberg has a commanding mastery of biblical studies, systematic theology, historical theology, philosophy, the epistemology of the sciences, and Lutheran tradition and ecumenism, as well as many other areas. Because his thinking is so subtle, sophisticated, and well-informed, two consequences follow. First, there is an urgent need for a medium-size single-volume of introduction to his thought, especially for English-speaking readers. Second, it would be inadequate to provide broad impressions of Pannenberg's work; we need many literal quotations of his own words. Accuracy is of paramount importance.

On this second point, I am heavily indebted both to Wm. Eerdmans Publications of Grand Rapids, U.S.A., and to SCM Press of London, U.K., for permission to quote many times from the English translations of Pannenberg's *Systematic Theology* and of his *Jesus—God and Man*. In this respect, I am grateful for constructive dialogue with Rev. Stuart Dyas and Rev. Dr. Tim Hull. In particular, Stuart Dyas, as before with other books, has carefully and meticulously checked proofs of the typescript, and often suggested improvements of clarity. My wife, Rosemary, has also checked proofs. All three have made helpful comments about language and style, to avoid undue complexity. I am grateful to Messrs Wipf and Stock, and for their Editor, Dr. Robin Parry, for their advice and speedy processing of this book's publication.

My high estimation of Pannenberg has been no recent flash in the pan. I have described my meeting with him in 1969, and our subsequent conversations. On 25th February 1972 I wrote about some of his work in the *Church of England Newspaper* under the title, "The Theologian Who Must Not Be Ignored." I discussed Pannenberg's work very positively in my book *The Two Horizons* (1980), and in *New Horizons in Hermeneutics* (1992). Finally, he visited us when I was Professor and Head of Department in the University of Nottingham to deliver the Firth Lectures. In 2013, I wrote some twenty pages on Pannenberg in my *Thiselton Companion to Christian Theology* (Eerdmans), of which I have repeated nothing below. It may seem absurd that I forgot to consult this earlier essay, but after twenty-seven books, it may not seem so ridiculous!

I hope that this book will help to hasten a new chapter in theology, focussed on Pannenberg's distinctive and massive achievements.

ANTHONY C. THISELTON, FKC, FBA,

Emeritus Professor of Christian Theology, University of Nottingham, and also the University of Chester, UK, and Emeritus Canon Theologian of Leicester and of Southwell and Nottingham

ABBREVIATIONS

ANF   *Ante-Nicene Fathers* (10 vols. Reprint. Grand
           Rapids: Eerdmans, 1993)

BDAG   W. Bauer, F. W. Danker, W. F. Arndt, and
           F. W. Gingrich, *A Greek-English Lexicon of
           the New Testament and Other Early Christian
           Literature* (3rd ed. Chicago: University of
           Chicago Press, 2000)

BQT   W. Pannenberg, *Basic Questions in Theology*
           (3 vols. ET. London: SCM, 1970–73)

HTR   *Harvard Theological Review*

JGM   Wolfhart Pannenberg, *Jesus—God and Man*
           (ET. London: SCM, 1968)

NIV   New International Version

NJB   New Jerusalem Bible

NPNF   *Nicene and Post-Nicene Fathers* (14 vols. Reprint. Grand Rapids: Eerdmans, 1993)

NRSV   New Revised Standard Version

SNTSMS   Society of New Testament Studies, Monograph series

ST   Wolfhart Pannenberg, *Systematic Theology* (3 vols. ET. Grand Rapids: Eerdmans, 1991, 1994, and 1998)

TDNT   *Theological Dictionary of the New Testament* (edited by G. Kittel and G. Friedrich. ET. 10 vols. Grand Rapids: Eerdmans, 1964–76)

TDOT   *Theological Dictionary of the Old Testament* (edited by G. Botterweck et al. 15 vols. ET. Grand Rapids: Eerdmans, 1987–2012)

TPS   Wolfhart Pannenberg, *Theology and the Philosophy of Science* (ET. Philadelphia: Westminster, 1976)

1

INTRODUCTION
LIFE, WORK, AND THOUGHT

1. THE SCOPE OF PANNENBERG'S WORK

IN MY OPINION, WOLFHART Pannenberg stands out as the most learned, creative, influential, and sophisticated theologian of the late twentieth century. Just as Karl Barth earlier turned back the tide of liberalism and anthropocentric thought in the earlier part of the century, so Pannenberg constitutes a turning point leading away from the thought of Rudolf Bultmann and his followers, and from existentialist theology.

If we compare Barth and Pannenberg, whatever the genius of Barth's fourteen English volumes of *Church Dogmatics*, Pannenberg's knowledge and expertise went well beyond his own massive three-volume *Systematic Theology* (ET, 1991–98, 1,676 pages). From systematic theology or doctrine, his work extended, first, to theories of knowledge and understanding, and hermeneutics (especially in his *Theology and the Philosophy of Science*, 1976, 456 pages, and *Basic Questions in Theology*, 3 vols., 1970–73, 700 pages). Second, his interest reached into Christology, with perhaps his most ground-breaking and original book constituting a new approach to that subject (*Jesus—God and Man*, ET, 1968, 458 pages). In the third place, Pannenberg worked in theological anthropology (notably in his *Anthropology in Theological Perspective*, ET, 1985, 552 pages, as well as in smaller books). Fourthly, he was meticulous and critical on the history of Christian thought from biblical times until today, as well as on philosophies of atheism and human self-centeredness. This included *Basic Questions* and many smaller works. These above works alone cover 7,386 pages, in addition to smaller works and many articles. To quantify his work, this may be less than Barth's fourteen volumes of *Church Dogmatics*, but his publications cover an immensely wider historical and interdisciplinary territory in very great depth.

2. PANNENBERG'S EARLY YEARS AND MAJOR INFLUENCES

Pannenberg was born in Stettin, then in Germany, now in Poland, in 1928. He was baptized in infancy in the Lutheran Church. At the time, however, he had little connection with the living faith of the church. In early January 1945, when he was sixteen, he underwent an intense Christian experience, which he later described as an experience of "light." He was returning from a piano lesson on a two-hour walk, and passing along a lonely woodland path, when he was "suddenly flooded by light, and absorbed in a sea on light."[1] Subsequently a Christian school teacher recommended that

1. Pannenberg, "God's Presence in History," 260–63.

he study the claims of Christian faith. He earnestly sought the meaning of life, and steadily underwent what many call a largely "intellectual conversion." This included a passionate belief in the resurrection of Jesus Christ. This has always featured at the center of his theology. He was also influenced in a positive direction for Christian belief through his love of music, and through his rejection of any supposed credibility of Friedrich Nietzsche's attack on Christianity.

From 1949 to 1953 he studied philosophy and some theology at the University of Göttingen, initially under Nikolai Hartman (1882–1950). At the same time, from 1948 to 1951, he studied theology and philosophy at Basel, firstly under the philosopher Karl Jaspers (1883–1969), and subsequently under the theologian Karl Barth (1886–1968). Barth remained a strong influence throughout Pannenberg's life. During his earliest years he also studied at Berlin and at Heidelberg, where he was influenced by Old Testament scholar Gerhard von Rad (1901–71), whom he regarded as his teacher, especially on history and tradition. He was also influenced by the philosopher Karl Löwith (1897–1973) on meaning in history.

In 1945–46 Hans von Campenhausen (1903–89) gave an influential lecture at Heidelberg on "Augustine and the Fall of Rome." This expounded Augustine's philosophy of history, and shed light on God's involvement with human history as-a-whole (*Historie*), in contrast to the sacred history (*Heilsgeschichte*) of many contemporary theologians. Hans von Campenhausen wrote that all the lines of history from the beginning converge toward a point in time and meet at Jesus Christ, in whom the meaning and goal of the whole movement are mysteriously unveiled. This theme had some place in Pannenberg's book *Jesus—God and Man*. It also paved the way for Pannenberg's theme of revelation in history, which we discuss below.

Pannenberg also became very strongly influenced by Edmund Schlink (1903–84), an orthodox Lutheran theologian, who emphasized the importance of doxology, confessional faith, and worship. He represented Lutheranism in the World Council of Churches and in the Ecumenical Movement in general. Schlink supervised Pannenberg's doctoral thesis at Heidelberg, which examined predestination in the works of Duns Scotus (d. 1308). Pannenberg submitted this in 1953, and published it in 1954. The theme of the divine sovereign purpose and decree remained a major component in many of his books, including *Jesus—God and Man,* his *Systematic Theology,* and other works. His *Habilitationsschrift* (post-doctoral qualification) in 1955 dealt with the relationship between analogy and revelation, especially in the context of God's knowledge. He became increasingly fascinated with, and influenced by, Karl Barth's thought concerning revelation and history. In philosophy and hermeneutics, he also became influenced by Hans-Georg Gadamer (1900–2001) and his book *Truth and Method* (1st German ed., 1960). More broadly and fundamentally he was greatly influenced by Georg W. F. Hegel (1770–1831), a philosophical giant, whose influence rivalled Kant's, especially on history, system, freedom, and the future.

In the late 1950s Pannenberg became closely involved with a group of contemporary post-doctoral-research scholars on apocalyptic. These included Klaus Koch (1926–), later Old Testament Professor at Hamburg, who wrote *The Rediscovery of Apocalyptic.* Others were Rolf Rendtorff (1925–2014), who wrote on the Old Testament and tradition, and his brother, Trutz Rendtorff (1931–2016), who wrote on ethics and society. Two more figures must be mentioned: Ulrich Wilckens (1928–), who wrote on apocalyptic and the New Testament, producing a New

Testament theology and work on the resurrection; and Dietrich Rössler (1927–), who also shared an interest in New Testament apocalyptic. In the late 1950s Pannenberg taught at Wuppertal Seminary, Berlin, with Jürgen Moltmann (1926–) and others. In 2009 Pannenberg called Moltmann "my dear friend and opponent." They held much in common, including especially eschatology, although they also held to differences.

3. SOME PERSONAL REMINISCENCES

To mention briefly a personal recollection, I first met Pannenberg at the Society for the Study of Theology in 1969. The highlight of the conference for me was that Pannenberg and his wife, Frau Hilke Pannenberg, were interested to see the City of Bristol, where we lived and taught, and answered positively with enthusiasm when we invited them to spend a few days in our Bristol home. This was an immensely stimulating time. I had completed a thesis on eschatology and the Holy Spirit in 1964, and since then had also become much involved in hermeneutics and the work of Hans-Georg Gadamer.

Pannenberg was an inexhaustible mine of information in both areas. Conversations were relaxed and very informative. He expressed passionate regret that a single philosopher, namely Martin Heidegger, had dominated German philosophy for so long. He appreciated much in Gadamer, but insisted that he constantly devalued the importance of propositions or assertions. We found great commonality in exploring further the consequences of taking full account of apocalyptic and eschatology. The personal reminiscences of Richard Neuhaus in his introduction to Pannenberg's *Theology and the Kingdom of God* certainly rang true for me. He commented, "Pannenberg speaks and writes not for an audience but for a companion. . . . He demands seriousness more than brilliance. . . . When he discovers the possibility of a serious intellectual exchange, a single conversation extends over several days."[2] Pannenberg possessed a burning passion for truth and understanding.

On the lighter side, the Pannenbergs invited us to dinner, with the opening question, "Where do you usually take your wife for dinner?" I managed not to admit that I had hardly ever taken my wife, Rosemary, out to dinner, and we spent some time discovering a suitable place for them to take us! In the event, it proved to be the first of several subsequent happy and instructive occasions. Pannenberg was also extremely generous in corresponding with me, including sending me several major books, which were all signed with the comment in German, "for Anthony Thiselton with warm good wishes," and, in the case of *Jesus—God and Man*, "with thanks for your hospitality."

Some years later, when I was Professor of Christian Theology in the University of Nottingham, where Pannenberg gave the Firth Lectures, lively conversations again took place. Also on the lighter side, we took him to see Newstead Abbey, home of Lord Byron. It soon became clear that he knew more about Byron's dates and whereabouts than the Newstead Abbey guides. One set of approving comments about his lovers evoked Pannenberg's sharp comment, "What about his wife?" His determination to see everything in the house and grounds did not take us near to our allotted time. But it provoked blunt protests from some staff or guides about allotted hours of employment, and frustrated expectations of leaving early!

---

2. Neuhaus, "Wolfhart Pannenberg: Profile of a Theologian," 18 and 19.

4. PANNENBERG'S UNIVERSITY APPOINTMENTS AND EARLIEST MANIFESTO IN ENGLISH

In 1961 Pannenberg became Professor of Systematic Theology at Mainz, and in 1968, he became Professor of Systematic Theology at the University of Munich until retirement in 1993, and then was also Emeritus Professor of Ecumenical Theology until his death in 2014. In America, he became Professor at the University of Chicago in 1963; at Harvard, in 1966; and at Claremont, in 1967. He was also elected a Corresponding Fellow of the British Academy, which was rare accolade awarded only to really outstanding scholars from overseas. Most of Pannenberg's key themes had emerged by 1959, at least in embryo, and were developed later in a huge flood of publications. Increasingly the resurrection of Jesus of Nazareth remained a central theme.

On 5th January 1959 Pannenberg delivered his early lecture—"Redemptive Event and History"—at Wuppertal, which was published in English in 1963, and again in 1970. He begins, "History is the most comprehensive horizon of Christian theology. All theological questions and answers are meaningful only within the framework of the history that God has with humanity, and through humanity with the whole of creation."[3] Pannenberg later wrote a paper entitled, "The Revelation of God in Jesus of Nazareth," published in German and English in 1967, which was designed to introduce Pannenberg's new and distinctive theology to a largely American and English-speaking audience. It was introduced by James Robinson, and elucidated aspects of his early first essay. In it he argues that history is moving towards a future that is as yet hidden, but that will be revealed. The title of the volume in which Pannenberg's

---

3. Pannenberg, "Redemptive Event and History," in Westermann, 314; and *BQT*, 15

essay appeared, *Theology of History*, implied an intentional contrast with Barth's "theology of the Word," and the entire school of Bultmann and his pupils.

In this respect there is a considerable convergence between the two early essays that Pannenberg produced. In both essays Pannenberg urged that his approach opposed on the one side Rudolf Bultmann (1884–1976) and Friedrich Gogarten (1887–1967) in their evaporation of history, and on the other side Martin Kähler's (1835–1912) *Heilsgeschichte* (salvation history) as history in the theological ghetto of personal experience. Pannenberg sees history as an indirect self-revelation of God. Bultmann, Pannenberg urges, "dissolved history into the historicity of existence; on the other side," Martin Kähler saw "the real content of faith as suprahistorical."[4] He similarly rejects Karl Barth's location of the incarnation of Jesus Christ in "pre-history" (*Urgeschichte*). He explains these trends as flights into the harbor of supposed safety from "the critical-historical flood tide," the harbor of supra-history or, with Barth, of pre-history. Critical historical investigation, he comments, often involves scientific verification of events, which does not seem to leave any room for redemptive events. Later in his essay, reprinted with an extended addition in *Basic Questions in Theology*, vol. 1, Pannenberg comments on "the anthropocentricity of the historical-critical procedure, which seems apt to exclude all transcendent reality."[5]

Pannenberg appeals forcefully to the Old Testament view of history. He rejected the notion of Mircea Eliade (1907–86) in his book *The Myth of the Eternal Return* that Israel sought refuge from history in some timeless mythical sphere. Israel, he insisted, had a thoroughly historical

4. Pannenberg, "Redemptive Event and History," in Westermann, 314.

5. Pannenberg, "Redemptive Event and History," *BQT*, 39.

understanding of reality. By way of contrast, he said, Israel is distinguished by the fact that it experienced the reality of its God not in the shadows of a mythical primitive history, but more and more decisively in historical change itself.[6] He insists that Israel's God can break into the course of his creation and initiate new events in it in surprising and unpredictable ways. Israel's faith includes the certainty that God again and again forms new acts, that he is a living God. This forms the basis for Israel's understanding of reality as a linear history moving toward a goal. It reflects the constantly creative work of God, which depends, in turn, on the structure of divine promise and fulfillment.[7] He appeals to the first developed concept of history in Israel's account of the successor to David's throne in 2 Samuel 7—1 Kings 2. In 2 Sam 7:1–16, God promises that Solomon will be successor to David's throne, and that this promise will be fulfilled. The Deuteronomist takes this further, beginning with Deut 7:8. The Book of Joshua emphasizes the fulfillment of God's promise through Israel's reclaiming the land.[8] Pannenberg concludes this section by commenting: "Thus Israel not only discovered history as a particular sphere of reality; it finally drew the whole of creation into history. History is reality in its totality."[9]

While he affirms the structure of promise and fulfillment as the framework of historical reality, Pannenberg turned to criticize Rudolf Bultmann's contrast between

6. Pannenberg, "Redemptive Event and History," *BQT*, 17; Westermann, 315.

7. Pannenberg, "Redemptive Event and History," *BQT*, 18; Westermann, 317.

8. Pannenberg, "Redemptive Event and History," *BQT*, 19; Westermann, 318–19.

9. Pannenberg, "Redemptive Event and History," *BQT*, 21; Westermann, 318.

history and eschatology in such a way that history is swallowed up by eschatology.[10] Bultmann, he argues, fatally leaves the apocalyptic picture of history out of account. In Pannenberg's view, the anticipation of the eschatological decision with reference to the person of Jesus does not mean the elimination of the futurity of the end. Without destroying this futurity, Jesus is the anticipated end, not the middle, of history.[11]

Bultmann saw the dehistoricization of history primarily in John, but also in Paul. But Pannenberg points to Paul's concern for history in Romans 9–11, and in counter-texts in John.[12] Both Israel and the Christian church look to "the one history which binds together the eschatological community of Jesus Christ and ancient Israel by means of the bracket of promise and fulfilment. Jesus is the revelation of God only in the light of the Old Testament promises."[13] *Promise* becomes a key category in Pannenberg, just as it does in the theology of Moltmann and Martin Luther (1483–1546). Pannenberg calls the promises of God in the Old Testament the "foundation" of the person and work of Jesus Christ.[14]

In contrast to his opposition to Bultmann, here Pannenberg appealed to biblical scholars Walther Zimmerli (1907–83), F. Baumgärtel, Gerhard von Rad, and Oscar Cullmann (1902–99) for the importance of hope and

10. Pannenberg, "Redemptive Event and History," *BQT*, 23; Westermann, 319.

11. Pannenberg, "Redemptive Event and History," *BQT*, 24; Westermann, 322.

12. Pannenberg, "Redemptive Event and History," *BQT*, 24–25; Westermann, 322–23.

13. Pannenberg, "Redemptive Event and History," *BQT*, 25; Westermann, 323.

14. Pannenberg, "Redemptive Event and History," *BQT*, 26; Westermann, 324.

promise, and for the contrast between promise and fulfillment. He invokes the philosophies of Karl Löwith and Wilhelm Kamlah (1905–76) for support in some directions,
including Löwith's work on the origin of world-history in
Israel. He also appeals to historians R. G. Collingwood
(1889–1943) and Wilhelm Dilthey (1833–1911) concerning their conceptions of history. Dilthey's notion that we
understand the meaning of events only in the light of the
end of history or the *end* of our lives became increasingly
important for Pannenberg's notion of history, meaning,
and wholeness.[15]

Pannenberg concludes that the anticipated coming of
the end of history now, in the midst of history, far from
doing away with history, actually forms the *basis from
which history as a whole becomes understandable*. He comments, "Christ's resurrection, daybreak of the eschaton, is
for our understanding and light which blinds, as Paul was
blinded on the Damascus road. . . . *The event of the resurrection . . . has broken through everything we can conceive of.*
. . . The freedom of the pure futurity of God is preserved.
. . . The fact [is] that this fulfilment, the end of history in
Jesus Christ, has *provisionally* already come."[16] The *total*
view of *reality as history* moves from *promise to fulfillment*.
Pannenberg comments, "The incomprehensibility of the
eschaton in history" has meaning "only in the framework
of a *universal historical understanding* of . . . reality." Pannenberg adds, "The sending [for mission] and history of the

---

15. Pannenberg, "Redemptive Event and History," *BQT*, 27–33;
Westermann, 329–33.

16. Pannenberg, "Redemptive Event and History," *BQT*, 37 (my
italics); Westermann, 333–35 (my italics). *BQT*, 38–80 constitute an
addition to the original essay.

eschatological community in the world can be understood only from this point of view."[17]

This concludes what was said in the original 1959 essay. We may now compare the later essay designed to introduce Pannenberg's distinctive theology to an English-speaking readership.

5. "THE REVELATION OF GOD IN JESUS OF NAZARETH": A "FOCAL ESSAY" FOR ENGLISH-SPEAKING READERS

James Robinson and John Cobb edited the volume *Theology as History* in their series New Frontiers in Theology. Pannenberg's essay in it, "The Revelation of God in Jesus of Nazareth," is described as the focal essay to introduce the work of Pannenberg to English-speaking readers. Pannenberg begins, "*In dealing with Jesus of Nazareth we are dealing with God himself.*"[18] He asks, how can we find *God* in *Jesus?*

(a) The first section concerns revelation, history, and Jesus. Pannenberg pointed out that Jesus stood in a specific tradition that expected the coming of the God of Israel. Jesus proclaimed the nearness of God's reign. Characteristic of his thought elsewhere is his utterance, "Jesus did not demand trust in his person without giving reasons for it."[19] This appeal to *argument*, reason, and evidence occurs throughout Pannenberg's thought.

Jesus claimed the *God* of Israel as his *authority*, a God already known to his hearers. He especially proclaimed the *nearness of God's reign* or kingdom. This exclusive concern for God's nearness and reign enables Jesus to pronounce

17. Pannenberg, "Redemptive Event and History," *BQT*, 37–38; Westermann, 335.

18. Pannenberg, "Revelation of God," 101 (my italics).

19. Pannenberg, "Revelation of God," 103.

forgiveness of sins upon those who opened themselves to his message of the nearness of God, or even upon those who trusted in him personally. The message of Jesus presupposed the expectation of God's future reign on earth. He shared the Israelite tradition of his hearers here. Pannenberg wrote that one cannot understand Jesus' claim unless one realizes its presuppositions, namely knowledge of God and the *anticipation of the future fulfillment* of God's will on earth. In an important sentence he asserts, "Israel's eschatological expectation was constitutive for Jesus's message to shared tradition."[20] Pannenberg expressed concern about the general history of religions, but *also* affirmed the particular and individual nature of the Christian proclamation. It does not concern some general notion of "god," but the *single God who is author of the world and* all reality.[21]

At this point Pannenberg expresses a characteristic comment: "Only in such a mental climate could God's message of God's future reign and of the meaning . . . be understood by non-Jews, or at least be translated into their own world of thought."[22] The two themes of *the kingdom of God* and the importance of an *apocalyptic frame of thought* constantly recur in Pannenberg's writings. He urged that the traditional anticipation of the coming reign of God became the decisive point in the proclamation of Jesus. The coming of Jesus transformed the Jewish tradition from within, while it transformed the non-Jewish conception of the one unknown God from without.

(b) In his second section Pannenberg examined the problem of the Hellenistic world and of non-Jewish readers today. He emphasized the need for the seeker himself to be transformed. He appealed especially to Paul's theology in

20. Pannenberg, "Revelation of God," 104.
21. Pannenberg, "Revelation of God," 107.
22. Pannenberg, "Revelation of God," 107.

Romans (not least to Romans 9–11) to argue that the Jew and the gentile face God on equal terms. Nevertheless, "The pre-eminence of the Israelite God over all other powers and interests" should be recognized in the hope for future realization of God's will on earth.[23] The God of Israel himself would confirm the message of Jesus, and only by anticipating this could his Jewish audience trust in him. Hence, the claim of Jesus was not an isolated and arbitrary one. A few may find difficulties in Pannenberg's emphasis on a "theology of religions," but he is deeply concerned to reveal the *universality* of the Christian message, and not to dissolve its *particularity* in Jesus Christ.

Pannenberg repeats, "The content of his [Jesus'] message was the general eschatological expectation of God's reign."[24] The delay of the *parousia* is no more than a theoretical problem. For he asserted, "Only in the light of the End is the close proximity of the Creator to his creation revealed, and hence the true nature of his creation."[25] The resurrection of Jesus relates to the general resurrection, because it is not a merely individual or isolated event. Pannenberg observes, "The expected general resuscitation of the dead at the End had already occurred in Jesus' case."[26] He did not use the term "resuscitation" in a literal, physical, sense. He acknowledged that speaking and thinking about a life on the other side of death is possible only in images and metaphors.

Nevertheless, Pannenberg takes the description of Jesus as "the firstborn from the dead" with utmost seriousness (Col 1:18; 1 Cor 15:20; Rom 8:29; Rev 1:5). He urges that the delay of the *parousia* did not cause a genuine crisis

23. Pannenberg, "Revelation of God," 111.
24. Pannenberg, "Revelation of God," 112.
25. Pannenberg, "Revelation of God," 113.
26. Pannenberg, "Revelation of God," 114.

in Christian faith, as some have suggested, because the resurrection of Jesus and his person assured Christians of their own future salvation. The attitude taken toward the message of Jesus and toward his person determined each person's final fate in the coming judgment.

(c) In his third section, Pannenberg focuses on the concept of revelation, and especially on the concept of *revelation as history*. He states, "Knowledge of God is made possible on a path guided by God himself—by a history— . . . already known to Israel."[27] "Fulfilment," however, is not straightforward. Often the *manner in which promises are fulfilled* may appear surprising, and be fulfilled in various ways. Few fulfillments, Pannenberg urges, may surpass an original meaning and take on a new meaning.

In the prophetic tradition, often the prophetic words are outstripped by events. Pannenberg wrote, "One has to reckon with an *intertwining* of both prophetic words and events. The event cannot be understood as an unessential appendage to the word."[28] Such early texts as 1 Kgs 22:28, on Micaiah, may remain fairly close to the prophetic tradition. However, in Deut 18:9–22 and Jer 28:6–9 the fulfillment goes far beyond the original prediction. Here Pannenberg writes, "It was no longer a single event, but a *whole* connected history that Yahweh had promised and was accomplished according to this promise."[29] Hence, apocalyptic texts may often embrace the whole of time from creation to the End.

In Pannenberg's words, "The eschatological event which binds history into a whole brings about final knowledge of God."[30] God's self-disclosure curves in and through

27. Pannenberg, "Revelation of God," 118.

28. Pannenberg, "Revelation of God," 120 (my italics).

29. Pannenberg, "Revelation of God," 121.

30. Pannenberg, "Revelation of God," 122–23.

history not simply through words: "God makes *himself* known through his deeds, and . . . the same thing is meant when it is said that his deeds make his *glory* known."[31] Ultimately God's final revelation cannot occur until the End of all history, and God's glory will be revealed in the face of Jesus Christ (2 Cor 4:6).[32] In the person and message of Jesus the most important titles include Son of Man, Messiah, *Kyrios* [Lord], Son of God, and *Logos* [the Word], which imply that the eschatological revelation of God is already anticipated in Jesus.

(d) In the fourth section, Pannenberg largely focuses on the relation between *faith and knowledge*, and between preliminary and final revelation. Jesus, he says, "can be understood to be God's final revelation only in connection with the whole of history as mediated by the history of Israel. He is God's revelation in the fact that *all history receives its due light from him*."[33] All the same, Pannenberg rejects the approach to the historical Jesus undertaken by positivism or Neo-Kantian dualism.

This refers in particular to the dualism associated with Bultmann that relegates the early Christian Easter message totally to the *significance* side of history. Bultmann understood the resurrection of Christ only as the *interpretation of Jesus' cross*. Pannenberg saw this as a splitting apart of historical consciousness, making God's revelation in Christ merely a *subjective* interpretation. He argued that this reflects an outmoded and questionable historical method. He writes, "Against this we must reinstate today the original unity of facts and their meaning."[34] He adds, "Whether or not Jesus was raised from the dead is a historical question

31. Pannenberg, "Revelation of God," 123.
32. Pannenberg, "Revelation of God," 124.
33. Pannenberg, "Revelation of God," 125 (my italics).
34. Pannenberg, "Revelation of God," 127.

insofar as it is an enquiry into *what did or did not happen at a certain time*. Such questions could be answered only by historical arguments."[35]

Pannenberg thus rejects the alternative "faith *or* knowledge" as "basically incorrect." These are not two alternative approaches. He writes, "Knowledge is not a stage beyond faith, but leads into faith—and the more exact it is, the more certainly it does so."[36] The act of faith or trust, he argues, *presupposes* a knowledge of the *trustworthiness* of the partner. He urges, "Christian faith must not be equated with a merely subjective conviction that would allegedly compensate for the uncertainty of our historical knowledge about Jesus. . . . Faith can breathe freely only when it can be certain."[37] This, he points out, does not imply rationalism, but, rather, respect for the personhood and activity of the biblical God. Pannenberg's early work on predestination, and the importance that he attached to divine decree and purposiveness in history, contributed to this point. He repeats, however, "This final self-demonstration of God is given to us only by way of anticipation of the coming general End for all men."[38]

(e) In his fifth and final section, Pannenberg reemphasizes the revelation of the *God of history*. He states, "Therefore it is only *from its End* that the *total reality* of the world will be complete."[39] He explains: "Once the world is understood as history, the origin of the All, who is also the End of history, becomes, as that End, the author of salvation which lifts man above the transitoriness of the present."[40] He

35. Pannenberg, "Revelation of God," 128 (my italics).
36. Pannenberg, "Revelation of God," 129.
37. Pannenberg, "Revelation of God," 131.
38. Pannenberg, "Revelation of God," 131.
39. Pannenberg, "Revelation of God," 132 (my italics).
40. Pannenberg, "Revelation of God," 133.

reaffirms that the *apocalyptic* notion of history is that which constantly hastens towards an End. To the present day, he urges, this is the only criterion of the truth of God's revelation in Jesus of Nazareth. If this is properly understood, theology will understand "the world as God's world, history as the field of his action, and Jesus as his revelation."[41] The pre-eminence and majesty of God as *Universal Creator*, Universal Source of life, *Universal Governor of History* and Universal Judge, who is revealed in Jesus Christ, constitutes a major theme in Pannenberg's thought, not only in this essay, but in virtually all of his works.

QUESTIONS FOR DISCUSSION

1. Why does Pannenberg stress that the resurrection of Jesus is not a merely individual or "isolated event" in the purposes of God?

2. Why does the fulfillment of God's promises sometimes take a surprising or unexpected form? Can we think of examples?

3. Advocates of the "Third Quest" for the historical Jesus tend to underline the context of the Israelite and Jewish tradition. What has Pannenberg particularly added to our understanding of this Jewish expectation?

4. Why is it important that Pannenberg stresses the unity of word and event in this tradition? To what extent does he have Bultmann's existential interpretation in mind?

41. Pannenberg, "Revelation of God," 133.

2

THE GOD OF ALL REALITY, THE THEISTIC "PROOFS," IMPLANTED KNOWLEDGE OF GOD, AND WORLD RELIGIONS

1. GOD AND ALL REALITY: THE UNIVERSALITY OF GOD AND THEOLOGY

(i) Four Initial Themes

PANNENBERG'S APPROACH TO THE doctrine of God begins with four themes. These concern the universality of God and theology; the importance of the finite and the particular; God's Lordship of history; and the general lack of knowledge among unbelievers or those of other faiths about an exact formulation for the identity of God.

(1) In 1963 Pannenberg gave a lecture entitled "The Crisis of the Scripture Principle," which was subsequently published in *Basic Questions in Theology*. We have cited parts of this in our Introduction. He writes,

> The task of theology goes beyond (some) special theme and includes all truth whatever. This universality of theology is unavoidably bound up with the fact that it speaks of God. The word "God" is used meaningfully only if one means by it *the power that determines everything that exists.* . . . It belongs to the task of theology to understand all being in relation to God, so that without God they [i.e. all being, *alles Seienden,* plural] simply cannot be understood. This is what constitutes theology's universality. A theology that remains conscious of the intellectual obligation that goes along with the use of the word "God" will try in every possible way to relate to all truth . . . to the God of the Bible, and to attain a new understanding of everything by viewing it in the light of this God.[1]

Pannenberg continues on the same theme, "It is only from its end that the total reality of the world will be complete. . . . Once the world is understood as history, the origin of the All, who is also the End of history, becomes, as that End, the author of a salvation which lifts man above the transitoriness of the present."[2] Several ideas call for comment. One is the theme of futurity and the incompleteness of our present finitude and the Christian church. Another

---

1. Pannenberg, *BQT,* vol. 1, 1–2 (my italics).
2. Pannenberg, "The Revelation of God in Jesus," 132–33.

is the retrospective, fuller understanding of God and reality from the future alone.

(2) All the same, this does not mean that we can ignore the *finite and the particular*. The finite and particular constitute a second theme in Pannenberg's approach to the doctrine of God. He also writes, "Men can approach God only through the world of finitude. Through the veil of the finite, men become aware of the infinite God. Therefore, their perspective is always one-sided and distorted. But at the *end* of the veiled way a revelation from God can occur, the self-unveiling of the God already provisionally known through . . . the veiling."[3]

(3) A third theme is implicit in the first, namely, as we have already observed, *God is a God of history*. Pannenberg continues to write, "Knowledge of God is made possible on a path guided by God himself—by a history . . . already known to Israel. . . . The basic *acts of Yahweh in history* were intended to make known to Israel the divinity of Yahweh."[4] Hence, from the very outset the three key terms of *God, history, and the End* (or eschatology) are inextricably bound together.

(4) Together with these major three themes, Pannenberg also considers *the unintelligibility of "God" for many people outside a Hebrew-Christian or theistic tradition*. He expounds this fourth theme in "The Question of God" (originally 1964). He concedes, "Anyone who tries to speak of God today can *no longer count on being immediately understood.* . . . Talk about the living God, the creator of the world, is threatening to become hollow today even on the lips of the Christian. The term 'God' seems to be dispensable."[5] Pannenberg considers the arguments

3. Pannenberg, "The Revelation of God in Jesus," 118.

4. Pannenberg, "The Revelation of God in Jesus," 118 (my italics).

5. Pannenberg, "The Question of God," 201 (my italics).

of Ludwig Feuerbach (1804–72) and Friedrich Nietzsche (1844–1900) that God was merely a human projection, and Martin Heidegger's (1889–1976) notion that we must be silent about God today.[6] He discusses the inadequacies of work by Bishop John A. T. Robinson (1919–83) and Herbert Braun (1903–91). Robinson became widely and popularly known for his book *Honest to God,* which attacked all "objective" belief in God in spite of his being a serious New Testament scholar. Robinson claimed to have drawn mainly on Rudolf Bultmann, Dietrich Bonhoeffer (1906–45), and Paul Tillich (1886–1965). Herbert Braun took the demythologizing programme of Bultmann even further, demythologizing even the reality of God. By contrast, Pannenberg regrets the limited appeal of much of Helmut Gollwitzer's (1908–93) work on believing in the existence of God only by faith.[7]

In his *Systematic Theology,* Pannenberg writes, "In modern secular cultures the word 'God' has increasingly lost this function (i.e., having a defined place), at any rate in the public mind."[8] He quotes Karl Rahner's (1904–84) comment that this word has become as enigmatic for us today as a *blank face.*[9] The concept of "God" has become unclear. Nevertheless, without this word, he says, the appeal for faith in Jesus of Nazareth loses its foundation. Hence, the Christian proclamation and faith cannot give up the word God.

Some ways of approaching a concept of God are simply unacceptable. For example, "The increase in grounding of faith in the experience of a guilty conscience came under such devastating criticism from the time of Nietzsche and

6. Pannenberg, "The Question of God," 202.

7. Gollwitzer, *The Existence of God as Confessed by Faith.*

8. Pannenberg, *ST,* vol. 1, 63.

9. Pannenberg, *ST,* vol. 1, 64.

Freud that we can hardly take this path today in trying to show the relevance of the Christian faith."[10] (Bonhoeffer, we should note, had already made this case well.)

It may be suggested that Pannenberg is too ready to acquiesce to the criticisms of Freud and others about the place of "guilt" than is needed, especially in his essay, "Protestant Piety and Guilt Consciousness." But his concern here is broad and against subjectivism. It reminds us of Krister Stendahl's (1921–2008) famous 1963 essay on Paul, in which he emphasized that Paul was less concerned about subjective feelings of guilt (for example, through conscience) than about our objective state of fallenness or alienation from God, whatever our feelings.[11] Pannenberg seeks to avoid any approach to God that is based on human subjective experience rather than on God's revelation. We need to begin, he says, with the broader concept of God. God is "behind" or "above" all encounters as a mysterious reality on which everything else depends. *God is the Other,* or Another.

(ii) Philosophical Theology and the Intelligibility of 'God'

In the biblical writings God is "solely a proper name," even if at times it also denotes a category of reality.[12] He is known and identified personally as "God"; but is also "God" in contrast to created and finite beings. The revelation of God in Jesus makes sense only in the light of the prehistory of the word. The difficulties in making what Christianity says about God *intelligible* today would become more difficult if Christian theology follows too hastily the cultural fashion

10. Pannenberg, *ST,* vol. 1, 65.

11. Stendahl, "The Apostle Paul and the Introspective Conscience of the West."

12. Pannenberg, *ST,* vol. 1, 68.

of retreating from metaphysics in philosophy. The rise of Logical Positivism would provide an example. Whereas religions may have originally assigned to the gods spheres of operation within a cosmic order, the decisive significance for the development of faith in Israel is belief in *one God*, which in general philosophical enquiry underlines.

The content of the word "God" does not derive from any *single* experience, or any single religious experience. If the word "God" is like a blank face to us, it reminds us by its very *strangeness,* or its lack of meaning in modern life, that "The theme of life's unity and totality is missing. . . . 'God' did in fact become a key word for awareness of the totality of the world and of human life."[13] Karl Barth had introduced the word "strange" in his essay "The Strange New World within the Bible." The development of Israel's faith to stress the worship of only one God, and the philosophical theology of the Greeks, were both pioneering, and helped to make the Christian message of revelation of the one God possible (1 Thess 1:9–10).

Philosophical theology emphasized, Pannenberg asserts, in opposition to a mythical tradition, "the unity, spirituality, immortality, and eternity of the design origin" (of the world).[14] He would agree with the theologians of the Second Vatican Council (1963–65) that philosophy is not only compatible with Christian theology, but also essential for its health. He concludes that one problem is the historical change of meaning which the term "natural theology" has undergone. When "natural theology" came to be used in contrast to "revealed theology," it came to mean "in accordance with human nature."[15]

13. Pannenberg, *ST,* vol. 1, 70–71.
14. Pannenberg, *ST,* vol. 1, 78.
15. Pannenberg, *ST,* vol. 1, 81.

Like Thomas Aquinas (1225–74), as well as Karl Barth, Pannenberg insists emphatically that theology is "the science of God." In the second article of Part 1 of his *Summa Theologiae,* Thomas insisted, "Christian theology should be pronounced to be a science . . . (even if) a higher science."[16] Pannenberg expounds this particularly in his book *Theology and the Philosophy of Science.*[17] In a comment reminiscent of Thomas F. Torrance (1913–2007), Pannenberg writes, "Theology derives its unity from its object," namely God.[18] He claims that God is the all-determining reality, which implies the close connection between theology and philosophy.

Pannenberg argues, "Transcendental philosophy, like ontological metaphysics, is always concerned with reality as a whole, which involves the double question of what the unity of existing things consists of . . . and what it is that makes all that exists a unity as a single reality."[19] Immanuel Kant (1724–1804) had introduced "transcendental philosophy," in contrast to empiricism and rationalism, to indicate not *"how* we know" but the very *possibility* and *grounds* of human knowledge. Yet within history, this reality-as-a-whole is always in process and unfinished before the End. Pannenberg concludes, *"The reality of God is always present only in subjective anticipations of the totality of reality, in models of the totality of meaning presupposed in all particular experience."*[20] God, he says, can be the object of investigation that claims scientific, and therefore intersubjective, validity.[21] The "scientific" status of theology entails

16. Aquinas, *Summa Theologiae,* vol. 1, Qu. 1, art. 2, 11.

17. Pannenberg, *TPS,* 295–345.

18. Torrance, *Theological Science.*

19. Pannenberg, *TPS,* 303.

20. Pannenberg, *TPS,* 310 (his italics).

21. Pannenberg, *TPS,* 326.

its use of cognitive propositions, and its ability to attest its truth-claims. He points out, however, that assertions about states of affairs have to do not only with facts but also with logic.[22] For example, in modern philosophy in his early *Tractatus*, Ludwig Wittgenstein (1889–1951) considers both "the propositions of natural science," which are open to empirical testing, and the logical constraints that definitions of words and tautologies imply. Logical Positivist A. J. Ayer (1910–89) also recognized this distinction.

On the question of the intelligibility of the word "God," once again the relative isolation of German philosophy from the Anglo-American analytical tradition becomes apparent. For example, Ian Ramsay (1915–72) explained the intelligibility of language about God in terms of "models and qualifiers." God is "wise" (model), but distinctively "infinitely" wise (qualifier). He is Father (model), but "heavenly" Father (qualifier).[23] However, Pannenberg is more aware than most German writers of this tradition, and addresses some of it elsewhere.

(iii) The Relevance of The Kuhn-Popper Debate and Metaphysics

Pannenberg considers verifiability within a horizon of effective communication. He evaluates the competing claims of Thomas S. Kuhn and Karl Popper, with their competing paradigms. Karl Popper (1902–94) argued that the sciences grow and progress by the step-by-step testing and falsification of hypotheses.[24] Thomas Kuhn (1922–96) drew attention to social and historical factors (e.g., the availability of apparatus and colleagues) that underlie scientific theories. Each historical era reflects dominant paradigms

22. Pannenberg, *TPS*, 331.

23. Ramsey, *Religious Language*.

24. Popper, *The Logic of Scientific Discovery*, 19–48.

of scientific discovery. He argued that the dominant models of paradigms constrain what counts as "testing" within a given paradigm. Practitioners share criteria, but these are relative to particular times and particular groups of persons. Kuhn observed that this is the context in which Karl Popper's notion of "falsification" became operative.[25] Their debate opens the discussion to include various kinds of evidence. In the end, Pannenberg concludes, "The presence of the all-determining reality in a *historical* phenomenon can be investigated only through an analysis of the totality of meaning implicit in the phenomenon."[26] He takes account of Kuhn's social and historical concern, but also Popper's concern about propositions.

In other words, Pannenberg certainly rejects crude positivism. But he urges that systematic and historical considerations can never be completely separated in theological study. Theological statements may be open to verification in relation to their claim to truth. Whether such verification may ever be brought to *final* conclusion remains a different matter. Hence, John Hick and Ian M. Crombie believe that while religious and theological statements are verifiable in principle, only the *eschatological future* can settle their verification.[27] We discuss this further in part 2 of this chapter, in section (ii).

These arguments broadly cohere with Pannenberg's *Metaphysics and the Idea of God.*[28] Part One of two parts, "The Idea of God," dates from lectures given in 1986. In his first chapter Pannenberg looks at Martin Heidegger's case

25. Kuhn, *The Structure of Scientific Revolutions.*

26. Pannenberg, *TPS*, 338 (my italics).

27. Pannenberg, *TPS*, 343; cf. Hick, *Philosophy of Religion*, 100–108, and Crombie, "Theology and Falsification."

28. Pannenberg, *Metaphysics and the Idea of God*, especially 3–109.

against metaphysics. Heidegger had originally intended to produce an ontology, but in view of the relativity of his notion of "being-there" (*Dasein*) in relation to the subject, and the radical conditioning of time, he abandoned this hope in his later work. He looked to poetry and art to provide hints of the ontology for which he had searched. Pannenberg concludes that Heidegger's case would mean abandoning the concept of God required by Christian theology.

Pannenberg rejects the claims of Auguste Compte (1798–1857), Friedrich Nietzsche, and Martin Heidegger that metaphysics must come to an end, as well as similar claims in a different tradition by the Logical Positivists. He claims, "In theology . . . the rejection of metaphysics cannot be successful over the long haul."[29] He argues that more than anything else, theological discourse about God requires relationship to metaphysical reflection if its claim to truth is to be valid.

Pannenberg turns in chapter 2 to the more recent debate about the nature of the Absolute, focusing on Friedrich Schleiermacher (1768–1834), René Descartes (1596–1650), and Immaneul Kant. G. W. F. Hegel (1770–1831), he argues, convincingly defended the primacy of the Infinite.[30] The remaining part of this section looks at the problem of self-consciousness, time, and eschatological ontology. The future remains so important for Pannenberg. Self-consciousness, he argues, cannot be used to explain its own origin. Further, he argues that Heidegger's view of time is individualistic and subjective or existential. Time can be defined only from the point of view of this or that participant.[31] Temporality (*Zeitlichkeit*) is the

29. Pannenberg, *Metaphysics and the Idea of God*, 5.

30. Pannenberg, *Metaphysics and the Idea of God*, 30–34, and 35–42.

31. Heidegger, *Being and Time*, Part II, sects. 67–71, especially

basis of time. In chapter 5 of *Metaphysics and the Idea of God*, Pannenberg argues, "Every assertion has an anticipatory structure. . . . Even metaphysical assertions are to be viewed in this sense as hypothetical and anticipatory, namely, as hypotheses that are directed toward reality as a whole."[32] This leaves room for Pannenberg's emphasis on both eschatology and reality as a whole.

2. THE THEISTIC "PROOFS"

Pannenberg concludes the section in which he considers arguments for the existence of God with the comment, "The arguments are not without significance as descriptions of the reality of humanity and the world which make talk about God intelligible and can thus establish criteria for it."[33] He considers the main historical philosophical theologians who have considered the arguments in their various forms. These include Augustine (354–430), Anselm (1033–1109), Aquinas, Descartes, G. W. Leibniz (1646–1716), Kant, and Hegel. The greatest *omission* from Pannenberg's discussion concerns, once again, Anglo-American analytical philosophy. This tradition includes the work of Alvin Plantinga (1932–), Norman Malcolm (1911–90), Charles Hartshorne (1897–2000), and, J. N. Findlay (1903–87), and many others.

(i) The Ontological Argument

Pannenberg begins by explaining that René Descartes put the ontological proof that Anselm had formulated on a wholly new foundation. In general, many eighteenth-century

_____

351–428.

32. Pannenberg, *Metaphysics and the Idea of God*, 94.

33. Pannenberg, *ST*, vol. 1, 95.

theologians resorted to defending the ontological argument by means of a further appeal to the cosmological line of argument. The cosmological argument proceeds from the *contingency* of worldly things to a cause of their existence. The first cause needs no other cause, but is "of itself" (Latin: *a se,* implying aseity).

This, Pannenberg argued, "was important in discussion of the ontological proof of Descartes because it led to the idea of a necessary being, which was the key to the proof, at any rate in a tenable form."[34] He continues, "The cosmological argument gave the thought of a necessary being objective validity until Kant claimed that to extend the idea of causality beyond the boundaries of the sensory world is illegitimate."[35]

Gottfried Leibniz argued in his *Monadology* (1714) that the ontological and cosmological arguments led to the concept of a *necessary* being by different paths. The thought of an absolutely perfect being, (i.e. One than which no greater can be thought) was the starting-point of the ontological proof in Anselm, and at first in Descartes. For Descartes the basic idea of the infinite was the same as that of perfection.[36] While Descartes had thought that we must define absolute perfection by necessary existence, Leibniz took the view that the two are identical.[37]

Pannenberg quite rightly adopts the view that Immanuel Kant has discredited the ontological argument, but states that his reason for doing so was primary to discredit the view that a *necessary* being could be *logically inferred* from contingent beings. On the other hand, Kant believed that the cosmological argument deserved respect, even if

34. Pannenberg, *ST,* vol. 1, 84.
35. Pannenberg, *ST,* vol. 1, 84.
36. Descartes, *Meditations,* 3, 28, 30.
37. Leibniz, *Monadology,* 45.

it, together with the ontological argument, transcended the bounds of strict formal logic.

In Anglo-American philosophy the key point is the notion that *existence is not a predicate.* The *concept* of God does not imply the *existence* of God. Pannenberg rightly asserts, "In his *Critique of Pure Reason* Kant undoubtedly destroyed the arguments of *speculative reason* . . . for the existence of a supreme being."[38] This includes strictly logical inference.

Descartes had said, "Existence can no more be separated from the existence of God than the truth that a triangle has three angles which add up to 180° can be separated from the essence of a triangle."[39] Ironically this let the cat out of the bag for Kant to formulate his most decisive objection to the argument. Descartes has in effect admitted that the truth of the ontological argument is simply the truth of definition. Kant asserted, "Being is evidently not a real predicate . . . something that can be *added to* the conception of a thing."[40] We should not say, "This orange is round and fresh, *and it exists*," as if "existence" were comparable with "round."

In the twentieth century Bertrand Russell (1872–1970) developed Kant's critique convincingly in terms of substituting what philosophers call an *existential quantifier* for the word "exists." To repeat: Kant does not consider the theistic proofs valueless, but insists that their *logic* is not infallible. Kant wrote, "There are . . . so many pseudo-rational principles that speculative reason seems . . . to have brought to bear . . . ."[41] However, theistic arguments may be respected as virtually intuitive insights.

38. Pannenberg, *ST,* vol. 1, 90 (my italics).

39. Descartes, *Meditations*, Meditation 5, 44–48.

40. Kant, *Critique of Pure Reason*, Book II, ch. 3, sect. 5, 368 (my italics).

41. Kant, *Critique of Pure Reason*, Book II, chapter 3, sect. 5.

However, the ontological argument has had its defenders in recent times. Alvin Plantinga , for instance, has drawn on the field of modal logic with its talk of "possible worlds" to craft a version of the argument that by-passes the objections of Gaunilo (994–1083), Kant, and Russell because it does not rely on the notion that existence is a predicate or a great-making property. Plantinga seeks to show that if it is *possible* that God exists then logically God *has* to exist. Other defenders include Norman Malcolm, Charles Hartshorne, and Hans Küng (1928–). In effect, this broadly accomplishes what Pannenberg is saying in his own way through the medium of Continental philosophy. Pannenberg writes, "The thought of God is thus indispensable for reason, even though we have not the slightest concept of . . . supreme perfection or of the necessity of existence."[42] He also claims that Hegel's renewal of the proofs of God no longer viewed the proofs as isolated theoretical constructs that prove the existence of God, but instead they express the elevation of the human spirit above sensory data. In spite of this, Pannenberg argues that Hegel also criticized the form of proofs of God insofar as they treated finite things as a solid starting point. The existence of God then became a dependent *inference* from this. Here is another resonance between Pannenberg and Plantinga.

(ii) Atheistic Critiques: Feuerbach, Marx, Freud, and Logical Positivism

Pannenberg also argues that the *anthropological interpretation* of the proofs of God's existence might also become the basis of an atheistic argument such as the one Ludwig Feuerbach promotes, according to which God is merely a human projection. This is because the thought of God may

42. Pannenberg, *ST*, vol. 1, 90.

be the expression of purely subjective needs such as the *projection of earthly human ideas,* or, in the case of Sigmund Freud (1856–1939) and Karl Marx (1818–83), a *human experience of guilt.*

Pannenberg regularly confronts Feuerbach's atheism elsewhere, including work in *Basic Questions in Theology.*[43] Ludwig Feuerbach had turned Hegel's philosophy on its head, replacing Spirit (*Geist*) with matter. Feuerbach drew on Hegel's "infinite consciousness" to argue that "consciousness of the infinite" was simply a human projection of God. Followed by Karl Marx and Sigmund Freud, he insisted that the God of religion and Christianity was entirely constructed by humankind. In Pannenberg's words, "The main intention of Feuerbach, as of his atheist successors Marx and Freud, was to unmask Christianity and the *Christian* idea of God as the product of human self-alienation."[44] He regarded God as a projection of human anxieties and longings. The key point that Pannenberg is eager to make is that the atheistic criticisms of Feuerbach, Marx, and Freud are *subjective ones,* i.e., they are based only on anthropological concerns of *human* nature.

In his *Anthropology in Theological Perspective,* Pannenberg maintains, "Feuerbach himself regarded religion as the very epitome of alienation, since in the idea of God human beings separate themselves from their own being . . . as though it were foreign to them, and then worship it. . . . The influence of Feuerbach and Marx in the discussion of the relation between religion and alienation has lasted down to the present time."[45] This influence is sometimes exerted

43. Pannenberg *BQT,* vol. 3, 86–94, "Anthropology and the Question of God"; and "Speaking about God in the Face of Atheistic Criticism," *BQT,* 100–115.

44. Pannenberg, "Speaking about God," *BQT,* vol. 3, 100.

45. Pannenberg, *Anthropology in Theological Perspective,* 275.

directly, while at other times it comes through the medium of Friedrich Nietzsche and Sigmund Freud, and through Émil Durkheim's (1858–1917) concept of reification. This concept refers back, again, to Feuerbach. He points out that as late as 1967 Peter Berger (1929–2017) was "still describing religion as alienated consciousness; in this context he understood alienation to be an objectification and reification of the products of human consciousness."[46] Feuerbach argued that humankind creates "God" in its own image.[47] One of his aphorisms was: "God was my first thought; reason, my second; humankind my third and last thought." Pannenberg is insisting that these critiques are all based on anthropology, in spite of Feuerbach's predictable reply that *of course* his atheism could only be based on anthropology!

Pannenberg finds no less difficulty in Nietzsche's and Freud's view which magnified the thesis of a neurotic origin of the idea of God in a sense of guilt.[48] He comments, "It is no accident that, at least since Feuerbach, modern atheism has concentrated its arguments upon anthropology, as can clearly be seen in Marx, Nietzsche, Freud, and [Jean-Paul] Sartre."[49] It is one thing, however, to distinguish between our conscious minds and what lurks beneath our minds in terms of the subconscious or unconscious. It is quite another to embed this in a purely mechanistic worldview, and to confuse speculative theories with authentic truth.

Freud grew up with no belief in God. In Vienna General Hospital he was drawn to neuropathology and psychiatry, and entered private practice in 1886. From the first he regarded mental processes as the "interplay of forces," on analogy with a machine. Hans Küng comments, "The

46. Pannenberg, *Anthropology in Theological Perspective*, 275.
47. Feuerbach, *The Essence of Christianity*, 12–32.
48. Pannenberg, *ST*, vol. 1, 104.
49. Pannenberg, *ST*, vol. 1, 105.

human *psyche* [was] understood as a kind of machine."[50]
He worked especially on hysteria, involved repressed guilt.
Many of his metaphors, such as "cathexis" were quasi-mate-
rialist notions. Therapy involved exploring the unconscious
through dreams and "double-meaning" expressions. On
this basis it is not surprising that he regarded religion as
the creation of inner conflict between conflicting drives.
Küng concludes, "Freud took over from Feuerbach . . . the
essential arguments for his personal atheism."[51]

In a totally different philosophical tradition, Pannenberg rightly rejects some of the more outrageous claims of
Logical Positivism, and more subtly the principle of falsification. Against the argument of A. J. Ayer that verification
constituted the criterion of truth and meaning, Pannenberg
cited Karl Popper's view that we can learn only by trial and
error. Our knowledge always begins with conjectures, models, hypotheses. Even immediate sense-perception contains
interpretation: all observation involves interpretation.[52] By
contrast, Ayer had maintained that as theology and ethics
cannot be tested by his empirical criterion of meaning they
were meaningless. He concluded, "The sentence 'there exists a transcendent God' has . . . no literal significance."[53]
More bluntly he dismissed such statements as "non-sense."
Only empirical and logical (true by definition) statements
have sense and meaning.

Pannenberg reveals his disdain for the rejection of metaphysics in the second part of his volume *Metaphysics and the
Idea of God*. He first reveals how "enriching" his encounter
with A. N. Whitehead's (1861–1947) philosophy had been,
with his metaphysics of "becoming" and "process-thought,"

50. Küng, *Does God Exist?* 268.

51. Küng, *Freud and the Problem of God*, 75.

52. Pannenberg, *Theology and the Philosophy of Science*, 37

53. Ayer, *Language, Truth, and Logic*, 158; cf. 7–13.

and explorations in relation to the totality of knowledge. He then looks at sense and reference as a question of logic and meaning in Gottlob Frege (1848–1925); and, finally, at meaning and the future in Wilhelm Dilthey. Dilthey followed Schleiermacher as a pioneer in hermeneutics, who, like Pannenberg, argued that meaning rested on a (often retrospective) understanding of the whole.[54]

Pannenberg rightly rejects Ayer's dated "fifth-form" or "basic" view of science as simple positivism. Indeed H. J. Paton (1887–1969) had dismissed this principle of verification as "simply positivism or materialism in a linguistic dress."[55] Pannenberg engages in a more sophisticated discussion of the principle of falsification. He concludes that, "Empirical checking of hypotheses takes place not within the framework of theoretically neutral observations, but normally as part of a process which could be described as 'paradigms articulation.'"[56] He cites Kuhn's further explanation that every problem that "normal" science sees as a puzzle can be seen, from another viewpoint, as a counter-instance and thus as a source of crisis and change. We have discussed Kuhn more fully above.

The British tradition of philosophy takes this discussion further in terms of the so-called "Invisible Gardener" analogy, which was suggested in the first instance by John Wisdom (1904–93) in his essay "Gods." John Wisdom told the story or parable of two explorers who came across what one regarded as a garden, and the other as an accidental sign of just possible, but doubtful, cultivation. They set tests to discover whether a gardener existed. Tests of sight, sound, and so on failed. Hence the doubter challenged:

54. Pannenberg, *Metaphysics and the Idea of God*, 113–29, 130–52, and 153–70, respectively.

55. Paton, *The Modern Predicament*, 39–40.

56. Pannenberg, *Theology and the Philosophy of Science*, 56.

would an invisible, inaudible, intangible, gardener be a real gardener at all? This debate was taken very much further in a discussion by three or four Oxford philosophers, which is reprinted in Antony Flew (1923–2010), *New Essays in Philosophical Theology*.[57] Does the parable depend on an anthropomorphic notion of "God"? Pannenberg, however, does not seem to engage with this explicitly British philosophical tradition.

(iii) The Cosmological Argument

Pannenberg insists that the cosmological argument—which tries to argue from dependent, caused things in the cosmos to an uncaused first cause—still remains important and relevant today. We must think of *God* as the *origin of the whole world.* He writes, "The cosmological argument, then, says something first about reason's demand for meaning, face-to-face with the world's contingency. It does at least make talk about God *intelligible*."[58] This coheres well with his emphasis on Greek traditions and other religions. This argument was formulated by Plato, Aristotle, and other ancient Greeks, by Maimonides (1135–1204) and many Jewish thinkers, by al-Kindi (d. 873), al-Ghazali (1058–1111), and most Islamic thinkers, and in Christianity by Aquinas, Duns Scotus (d. 1308), and many others.

In Islamic thought, the *kalām* version of the cosmological argument, as other versions, distinguishes between a necessary Being—a Being that *cannot not* exist—and contingent, dependent beings, which can either exist or not exist. It argues that without a necessary Being as First Cause one cannot account for the existence of contingent beings. With Pannenberg, its exponents discuss the difference between

57. Flew (ed.) *Essays in Philosophical Theology*, 47–56 and 71–75.
58. Pannenberg, *ST,* vol. 1, 94 (my italics).

ontingency and necessity. God is God's own ground, and controls all things. In Jewish tradition Maimonides followed the biblical accounts of creation in articulating his version. Thomas Aquinas set forth the cosmological argument in three of his "Five Ways." The first "Way" of establishing belief in God's existence takes up Aristotle's argument from potentiality (or movement, Latin, *motus*) to actuality. The second "Way" considers efficient cause. The third "Way" examines contingency and finitude.

In more modern times, Samuel Clarke (1675–1729) defended the cosmological argument in the light of scientific advances, and considered the chain of secondary causes, arguing that "the whole" cannot constitute a "necessary" cause—lots of contingent things do not add up to a necessary thing.[59] David Hume (1711–76) challenged the assumptions of the argument, replacing "cause" by "constant conjunction," arguing, "Upon examination . . . the necessity of a cause is fallacious and sophistical."[60] Kant pressed criticisms of cause even further. In more recent times, William Lane Craig (1949–) defended the argument in the light of the finite history of the world and G. E. M. Anscombe (1919–2001) and Herbert McCabe (1926–2001) have exposed fallacies in Hume's arguments about "cause."

While he places more emphasis on the ontological argument than the cosmological argument, Pannenberg, not surprisingly, is more concerned with *a priori* knowledge of God, than with conclusions that rest on a chain of inferences. Further, he argues that the ontological argument is more prominent in current discussions. Nevertheless, he regards the cosmological argument as relevant because it draws inference "from the contingency of worldly things to a cause of their existence which needs

59. Clarke, *A Discourse concerning Natural Religion*.
60. Hume, *A Treatise of Human Nature*, 79–94.

38

no other but is of itself."[61] God is the author of order.[62] Virtually all of the terms in modern debate have a serious place in Pannenberg's arguments.

3. A CRITIQUE OF NATURAL THEOLOGY, AND "IMPLANTED" KNOWLEDGE OF GOD

(i) Natural Theology

Pannenberg now undertakes a critique of natural theology. He first examines different meanings of the term itself, largely on the basis of Rom 1:18–20 and 2:14. Paul argues that knowledge of the divine law necessarily carried with it knowledge of God and the duty of worshipping him. However, the natural religion of the Enlightenment suggested that a theism based on natural reason was the original religion of the race. David Hume criticized this assumption, claiming that human passions, not reason, had supposedly generated religion.[63]

On the other hand, Friedrich Schleiermacher argued that in spite of the multiplicity and diversity of religions, the immediacy of dependence upon God constituted the heart of religions naturally. Albrecht Ritschl (1822–89), however, rejected the metaphysical basis of the concept of God, which implied rejection of the patristic reception of the metaphysical doctrine of God.[64] Ritschl's attempt to avoid metaphysics was based on an apologetic concern to free religion from the scientific positivism of his age. Unfortunately, in Pannenberg's view, Karl Barth attacked natural theology on a similar basis to Ritschl. Barth regarded natu-

61. Pannenberg, *ST,* vol. 1, 84.
62. Pannenberg, *ST,* vol. 1, 86.
63. Pannenberg, *ST,* vol. 1, 97.
64. Pannenberg, *ST,* vol. 1, 98–101.

ral theology as a product of human self-preservation and self-affirmation. Perhaps against his ultimate intentions, Barth played into the hands of Feuerbach, aspects of whose thought he admired, by implying that natural religion could be the product of a human projection of "God."

Pannenberg considers Barth's contention that the whole development of modern Protestant theology is in line with Feuerbach, with its focus on humanity and its awareness of God. By the end of the eighteenth century, the rational theology of the Enlightenment had lost its cogency. All the same, the possibility of proving an anthropological need for rising above the finite to the thought of the infinite and absolute, Pannenberg claims, "still has significance for the truth-claim of all religious talk about God."[65]

(ii) Implanted Knowledge of God

In a more important comment, Pannenberg writes, "The idea of an inborn knowledge of God in the soul has been common to the theology of the Christian West from the time of Tertullian [160–220]. It was never abandoned in the Augustinian tradition of mediaeval theology. . . . Even Thomas . . . admitted that a certain form of knowledge of God, although confused (*sub quadam confusione*), is implanted in us by nature."[66] He adds many others who support this reading of Romans, including Martin Luther and Philip Melanchthon (1497–1560). Admittedly reason became distorted by the fall, but implanted knowledge of some kind remains.

Pannenberg respects what he calls a primordial awareness of God, or a religious *a priori*. But this is not in the

65. Pannenberg, *ST,* vol. 1, 106.

66. Aquinas, *Summa Theologiae*, Pt. 1, Qu. 2a, art. 1, ad 1; quoted by Pannenberg, *ST,* vol. 1, 108.

same sense as Rudolf Otto's (1869–1937) "Wholly Other"
or *mysterium tremendum*. In his *Idea of the Holy* (1923),
Otto described this "creature-feeling" as ranging from
"intoxicated frenzy" to "grisly horror and shuddering."[67]
Whereas Otto devalues the rational, Pannenberg insists
that such religious feelings are "always mediated by perception of facts."[68] For similar reasons he dissociates himself
from Anders Nygren's (1890–1978) view of the Eternal as
the basic transcendental category of religion. Pannenberg
returns to Paul, except that, for him (following Gerhard
Ebeling [1912–2001]), Rom 1:20 differs from Rom 2:15.
In Rom 1:20, Paul speaks of drawing inferences from creation. However, Rom 2:15 comes near to speaking of moral
law and conscience.[69]

4. WORLD RELIGIONS, AND OUR EXPERIENCE OF THE WORLD

(i) Other Religions Are Not Merely Idolatry

On the experience of religions, Pannenberg argues that *we
cannot simply dismiss them as sheer idolatry*. However, this
is not one of his clearest chapters. His starting-point is the
religious nature of humanity, *in which God has planted some
knowledge of himself*, even if this is confused and open to
distortion. If, as Aquinas also believed, such knowledge is
often confused and distorted, it will be inevitable that in-
consistencies and contradictions will arise, and these may
lead to refinements, including assessments of whether the
supposed deities can deliver what they have claimed for
themselves. Hence, attempts to attend to this *implanted*

67. Otto, *The Idea of the Holy*, 12 and 13.
68. Pannenberg, *ST*, vol. 1, 115.
69. Ebeling, "Theological Reflections on Conscience," 412.

knowledge may lead to an understanding of the purity of monotheism, and ultimately to an understanding of Christian revelation. Before the End, mistakes and misunderstandings still exist within the fallible church.

With Barth, Pannenberg underlines the primacy of God and his self-revelation in contrast to merely human feelings of need or subjective guilt.[70] Pannenberg begins by pointing out that Augustine had argued that knowledge of God was inseparable from worship of God.[71] We must evaluate the difference between true and false religion in the face of religious plurality. Hegel, Schleiermacher, and Ernst Troeltsch (1865–1923) all reflect insights and mistakes. Yet we cannot, Pannenberg argues, detach the concept of God from that of religion: "These anthropological definitions are certainly not totally false."[72] Schleiermacher's work on religion at least opened a deeper understanding of the finite.[73]

(ii) The Variety of Religions and Monotheism

In an important statement Pannenberg urges, "Defining the nature of religion does not answer the question of its *truth*, or of the truth of the theses which are believed and handed down in the various religions."[74] Nevertheless, in one form or another religion is a constitutive part of human nature, which can be seen in its universal occurrence from the very beginnings of humanity. Pannenberg writes, "The universal presence of religious themes corresponds to the feature of human behavior that is described as openness to

70. A summary of his views is well presented by Stanley Grenz in *Reason for Hope*, 21–25.

71. Pannenberg, *ST*, vol. 1, 121.

72. Pannenberg, *ST*, vol. 1, 138.

73. Pannenberg, *ST*, vol. 1, 139–44.

74. Pannenberg, *ST*, vol. 1, 151 (my italics).

the world, ex-centricity [or looking beyond a worldview centered on entirely and narcissistically on oneself], or self-transcendence."[75] On the one hand, we cannot rule out the possibility that the religious disposition may actually be entangling us in what Pannenberg calls a natural illusion. On the other hand, in the case of a religious disposition by nature, we are "incurably" religious.[76] The contingency of everything finite postulates "a self-existent Origin or Author of the world."[77]

Pannenberg considers specifically the development of religion in the Greeks, in ancient Israel, and elsewhere, and the approaches in modern thought of Schleiermacher, Hegel, and others. He believes that "The manifestation of divine reality even within the unresolved conflicts of religious and ideological truth claims is called revelation."[78] *This does not imply that all religions are authentic.* But Pannenberg refuses to condemn outright approaches of non-Christian religions. He writes, for example, "The Jewish polemic against the belief in God among other peoples which Paul was adopting in Romans was one-sidedly assessing the perverting of the incorruptible God into the image of corruptible things."[79]

It is scarcely surprising that some critics express reservations about Pannenberg's position from both sides. He himself acknowledges that there is an "ambivalence" in the position that he holds. He appeals to the value of a balanced and critical philosophy of religion. Pannenberg argues that Paul's criticism is not directed against the fact that the incorruptible power of God *is perceived* in the structures

75. Pannenberg, *ST,* vol. 1, 155.
76. Pannenberg, *ST,* vol. 1, 157.
77. Pannenberg, *ST,* vol. 1, 159.
78. Pannenberg, *ST,* vol. 1, 171.
79. Pannenberg, *ST,* vol. 1, 179.

of creation. Paul's criticism is that we depict the power of God *according to the image of corruptible things*, and thus confuse God with his creatures (Rom 1:25).

5. GOD'S SELF-REVELATION

(i) God Makes Himself Known

Pannenberg's discussion of religions leads on to a further discussion of *the revelation of God*. He states, "Human knowledge of God can be a true knowledge that corresponds to the divine reality only if it originates in the deity itself. God can be known *only if he gives himself to be known*. The loftiness of the divine reality makes it inaccessible to us unless it makes itself known."[80] Such a statement is clearly reminiscent of Karl Barth and his emphasis on God's "readiness to be known," and to the majestic transcendence of the sovereign God.

Pannenberg traces the notion of revelation through several biblical-historical events, from earlier years until the exile. The concept of revelation came to be associated with the *future* divine self-demonstration. The varying words and thought forms of biblical witnesses who speak of divine revelation cannot be denied. We must evaluate the multiplicity of the biblical statements about revelation. In Pannenberg's view, Gerald Downing (1935–), who considers that the concept of revelation is not fully supported in the Bible, and is grossly overvalued, does not make his case with sufficient precision.[81] Sometimes revelation is associated with command, directive, or law; at other times it may be associated with the divine Spirit or the hand of God, as in Ezekiel. The famous declaration of God's self-disclosure to

80. Pannenberg, *ST,* vol. 1, 189 (my italics).

81. Downing, *Has Christianity a Revelation?*

Moses in Exodus 3 is not exactly God's self-revelation in a precise sense, for what it amounts to can be seen only in the unfolding history and action of God, in accordance with his promise. God's final manifestation is still hidden.[82]

Pannenberg cites the many passages in the Synoptic Gospels when Christ says, "Nothing is covered that will not be revealed" (Luke 13:2; Matt 10:26). Paul expresses the very same idea in his declaration that Christians are to judge nothing before the time when Christ will return to judge (1 Cor 1:7; 4:5). He comments, "What is now hidden with God will be made manifest only in the end-time."[83] In 1 Cor 2:7–9, he points out, the apocalyptic term "mystery" is used for the plan of salvation according to the wisdom of God. In broad terms, the Prologue to John's Gospel (John 1:1–14) and the opening sentences of Hebrews (Heb 1:1–2) show how revelation comes with the incarnation of Christ.

Pannenberg also discusses the function of the concept of revelation in the history of theology. He begins with the Apostolic Fathers, Justin (100–165), and Irenaeus, and notes how Origen (184–253) quotes 2 Tim 3:16 in support of the view that the Scriptures which predicted the appearing of Jesus Christ, were inspired by the Spirit. In Origen, he observes, "[w]e already have a view of revelation which understands the inspiration of the biblical writings as revelation."[84] Yet with the Middle Ages the concept of revelation changes primarily into appeals to the church.

Again, another change comes with the Enlightenment, its criticism of authority, and its attack on the verbal inspiration of the Bible. Pannenberg particularly examines the work of Hegel and J. G. Fichte (1762–1814). Fichte had redefined revelation as an introduction to a *moral* religion.

82. Pannenberg, *ST*, vol. 1, 207–8.
83. Pannenberg, *ST*, vol. 1, 209.
84. Pannenberg, *ST*, vol. 1, 217.

More recently Martin Kähler focused the concept of revelation more specifically on the person of Jesus Christ, which led in turn to Karl Barth's notion of the three forms of revelation in terms of the Word *written*, the Word *preached*, and the Word *enfleshed*, Jesus Christ himself.

(ii) Different Views of Revelation in Theology

Pannenberg then examines *views of revelation* in a recent and current context. He looks especially at the work of James Barr (1924–2006) and William Abraham (1947–), as well as that of Karl Barth. With many qualifications, he emphasizes, "I am *not* saying that it is biblically inappropriate to speak of God revealing himself in his Word. My point is that this thesis needs more nuanced biblical justification than can be given by simply adducing John 1:1 and Heb. 1:1–2."[85] He quotes Gerhard Ebeling for rightly demanding that we should not "play-off" the notion of "Word of God" against "revelation," as if these were rival concepts. In positive terms, he finds the idea of personal communication constructive and attractive in this context.

Pannenberg concedes that the argumentative appeal to the Word of God has been hampered both by the often unduly authoritarian style of theological argument and the development of the historical-critical method of biblical study, which elsewhere he regards as anthropocentric. His fundamental positive point is: "The future summation of world history which is connected with the coming of God's kingdom that will end all human rule, with the judgment of all human injustice, with the transformation of the present creation, and with the resurrection of the dead, will finally also make God's deity and divine glory manifest to 'all flesh.'"[86]

85. Pannenberg, *ST,* vol. 1, 237 (my italics).

86. Pannenberg, *ST,* vol. 1, 246.

This takes account of the fact that the divine Word, again, includes direction, command, or law, as well as declarations, propositions, and the manifestation of God. It accords with "the biblical understanding of the divine Word," which is in turn related to divine Wisdom, and the *Logos* concept. Pannenberg concludes, "Jesus Christ, then, is the Word of God as the quintessence of the divine plan for creation and history and of its end-time."[87]

In our next chapter we shall consider, also under the doctrine of God, God's Trinitarian nature, and his character or attributes.

QUESTIONS FOR DISCUSSION

1. What does Pannenberg mean by the universality of God, and the universality of theology?

2. How does Pannenberg address the problem for some of the "unintelligibility" of God? Would a supplement to his answer from Anglo-American philosophy be helpful?

3. Why is it insufficient to ground faith in God in the experience of a guilty conscience?

4. What does he mean by speaking of "ontological metaphysics"? Why is this important?

5. What is the relevance of the debate between Kuhn and Popper to Pannenberg's theology?

6. Why does Pannenberg seem to use the word "contingency" so frequently?

87. Pannenberg, *ST,* vol. 1, 257.

3

GOD AS TRINITY AND HIS ATTRIBUTES

1. GOD AS FATHER, SON, AND HOLY SPIRIT

(i) God's Fatherly Care

PANNENBERG INSISTS AGAIN AND again that the heart of the message of Jesus was the nearness of God's reign.[1] God shows himself to be Father, especially the heavenly Father who cares for his creatures (Matt 6:26; Luke 12:30). He causes his sun to shine and rain to fall on the just and the unjust (Matt 5:45). He is a model of love for enemies, which Jesus taught (Matt 5:44–45). He is ready to forgive those who turn to him (Luke 15:7, 10). Pannenberg writes, "God's fatherly goodness is related to his [Jesus'] eschatological message of the nearness of the divine rule."[2] In addition to

1. Pannenberg, *Theology and the Kingdom of God*, 51–64.
2. Pannenberg, *ST*, vol. 1, 259.

this, Pannenberg observes, "The God of Jesus is none other than the God of Jewish faith according to the witness of the Old Testament. He is the God of Abraham, Isaac, and Jacob (Matt. 12:26–27), the God whom Israel confesses in the *shema* of Deut. 6:4."[3]

Pannenberg adds that the intimacy implied by invoking God as *Abba* typifies the relation of Jesus to God. Like Barth, he regards God's eternal election of Jesus Christ as a fundamental part of his purpose. He comments, "The fatherly relation of God to the king by an act of adoption gave the idea of God as Father a consistency which made it much more than a metaphor."[4] The church of the New Testament often appealed to such passages as Ps 110:1 for the notion that Jesus is crowned as God's adopted Son.

Many may regard the language about the relationship between Jesus and God as Father as purely time-bound. Nevertheless, Pannenberg observes, "On the lips of Jesus, 'Father' became a proper name for God. It thus ceased to be simply one designation among others. It embraces every feature in the understanding of God which comes to light in the message of Jesus. . . . The words 'God' and 'Father' are *not just time-bound concepts* from which we can detach the true content of the message."[5] This concept, he insists, is one of the starting-points for the history of primitive Christian Christology.

(ii) God, Jesus, and Sonship

This relationship is echoed by Paul in Rom 1:3–4, where Paul says that Jesus was declared to have the dignity of divine sonship. Pannenberg also insists that the idea of

3. Pannenberg, *ST,* vol. 1, 260.
4. Pannenberg, *ST,* vol. 1, 261.
5. Pannenberg, *ST,* vol. 1, 262–63 (my italics).

the pre-existence of Jesus does not contradict the fact that his divine sonship will be revealed only as eschatological, or at least from the time of his resurrection. God raised Jesus from the dead as Lord or *Kyrios*. The pre-Pauline and Pauline communities regularly used the title *Kyrios* for the exalted Lord Jesus. Pannenberg believes, "The title *Kyrios* implies the full deity of the Son. In the confession of Thomas in John 20:28 the titles God and Lord are expressly set alongside one another."[6]

Paul, especially argues in Romans, that the Holy Spirit of sonship was given to all Christians (Rom 8:15), and this same Holy Spirit is the one who declared Jesus as divine Son. All sonship, Pannenberg says, rests on the working of the Holy Spirit (Rom 8:14). In company with Jürgen Moltmann (and later also Eugene Rogers), citing especially the narrative of the baptism of Jesus by the Holy Spirit as well as in the infancy narratives, he sees the first fundamental theme of an exposition of the Holy Trinity in the narrative of the Gospels.[7] In the event of the baptism of Jesus, all three persons of the Trinity were active: God the Father signified his pleasure at the baptism of Jesus; Jesus Christ submitted to baptism; the Holy Spirit descended upon Jesus visibly as if in the form of a dove. The event then inaugurated the messianic ministry of Jesus, which began when the Holy Spirit led him into the wilderness to be tested or tempted. This visibly demonstrated the fellowship of Jesus as Son, with God as Father, in the power of the Holy Spirit.

6. Pannenberg, *ST,* vol. 1, 266.

7. Pannenberg, *ST,* vol. 1, 266; Moltmann, *The Spirit of Life,* 60–73; Rogers, *After the Spirit,* 98–171.

(iii) God's Self-Differentiation, and Persons as Relational

To Pannenberg one important factor was the self-differentiation of God as Father, Son, and Holy Spirit. This was eventually understood, at least in history, as a hypostatic differentiation (i.e., one of substance, or actual, concrete existence). He writes, "The Risen Lord is so permeated by the divine Spirit of life that he himself can be called a life-giving Spirit (1 Cor. 15:45)."[8] Pannenberg then traces the doctrine of the Trinity through the second and third centuries, noting the reference of Irenaeus to the Son and the Spirit as the "two hands" of God, the notion of three different spheres of operation in Origen, and the further development in Athanasius (296–373), Basil of Caesarea (330–79), and Gregory of Nyssa (335–94).

The argument of Athanasius coheres well with Pannenberg's insistence that "Father," "Son," and "Spirit" are essentially *relational terms*. Athanasius insists that "the Father would not be the Father without the Son and therefore that he was never without the Son."[9] The Cappadocian Fathers took up the same line of thinking, attempting to define the distinctiveness of the persons of the Trinity.

Pannenberg then engages in a more detailed discussion of the doctrine of the Trinity in dogmatic theology. He begins with the prior understanding of God alone as the Supreme Being (Exod 3:14), and of God as Spirit (John 4:24). In the history of the church he examines especially Peter Lombard (1100–1160) in his *Sentences* in the Middle Ages. He then argues, "Reformation theology lost the tighter systematic structuring that the doctrine of God had achieved in High Scholasticism, because it took seriously

8. Pannenberg, *ST,* vol. 1, 269.

9. Athanasius, *Contra Arian*, 1.29; cf. Pannenberg, *ST,* vol. 1, 273 and 279.

its own declaration that the Trinity is known only by revelation. This meant that it had to base what it said about the Trinity on holy Scripture."[10] With the doctrine of the Trinity, God and his revelation are at the heart of Christian theology. He comments, "In its awareness of the central function of this doctrine, the speculative theology of the 19th century helped to renew it after the manner of Hegel."[11] He concludes, "To find a basis for the doctrine of the Trinity we must begin with the way in which the Father, Son, and Spirit come on the scene and relate to one another in the event of revelation."[12]

Pannenberg believes that when we are enquiring into the distinction and unity of the divine persons, our starting point should always be with the person of Jesus Christ. We then discover the reciprocal self-distinction of the Father, Son, and Spirit, which is the concrete form of Trinitarian relations. He cites Matt 11:27, "No one knows the Father except the Son and anyone to whom the Son chooses to reveal him." Similarly, in John 14:6 Jesus says, "No one comes to the Father, except through me."

In terms of the reciprocal relationship between Jesus and God, Jesus says in John, "I glorified you on earth, by finishing the work that you gave me to do" (John 17:4). Pannenberg observes, "Precisely by distinguishing himself from the Father, by subjecting himself to his will as his creature, by thus giving place to the Father's claim to deity as he asked others to do in his proclamation of divine Lordship, he allowed himself to be the Son of God and one with the Father who sent him (John 10:30)."[13] Certainly Christ

10. Pannenberg, *ST*, vol. 1, 289.

11. Pannenberg, *ST*, vol. 1, 293.

12. Pannenberg, *ST*, vol. 1, 299.

13. Pannenberg, *ST*, vol. 1, 310.

is "Lord," who "must reign until he has put all his enemies under his feet" (1 Cor 15:24–25).

Following Donald Baillie (1887–1954), Pannenberg comments, "Nor can the Father be thought of as unaffected by the passion of his Son if it is true that God is love. . . . We may speak of the Father's sharing the suffering of the Son, his sym-pathy [joint-fellow-suffering] with the passion."[14] The resurrection of Jesus is not only an act of the Son of God himself (where Jesus as Life-giver in John raised himself from the dead), but (mainly elsewhere in New Testament) an act of *God in the power of the Holy Spirit*. Pannenberg agrees with Augustine that the Spirit is the bond of union between the Father and the Son. The Spirit *proceeds* from the Father and the Son (John 15:26), in spite of the Eastern Orthodox criticism of the *filioque* ("and the Son") clause.

In contrast to Karl Barth, Pannenberg regards the notion of understanding the Trinity in terms of different modes of being of one subject as inadequate. By contrast, he calls the persons of the Trinity "separate centres of action." The three persons "constitute the different distinctions of the persons. . . . The persons cannot be identical simply with any one relation."[15] He observes, "Only of the Son may we say that the other person from whom he distinguishes himself, i.e. the Father, is for him the only God, and that the Son's own deity is grounded in the fact that he thus subjects himself to the deity of the Father. The Spirit, of course, also shows his deity by teaching us to recognize and confess the Son as Lord (1 Cor. 12:3)."[16]

In contrast to Moltmann, Pannenberg avoids a notion of the so-called "Immanent Trinity," with the perichoretic mutuality of the personal relations within the life of

14. Pannenberg, *ST,* vol. 1, 314.
15. Pannenberg, *ST,* vol. 1, 319–20.
16. Pannenberg, *ST,* vol. 1, 321.

the Trinity.[17] He comments, "Only because the communion of the persons finds its content in the monarchy of the Father as a result of the common working can we say that the Trinitarian God is none other than the God who Jesus proclaimed, the heavenly Father whose reign is near, dawning already in the work of Jesus."[18] In his monarchy, the Father is one God.

To sum up: Pannenberg's key category is self-differentiation, which allows each person of the Trinity to be themselves and one in will, with the proviso that the Father is more the Father in relation to the Son; the Son is more the Son, in relation to his Father; and the Holy Spirit is more the Spirit in relation to the Father and the Son. Although Hegel used the term "self-differentiation," Pannenberg develops it in a different way from Hegel. Unlike Moltmann, this scheme still allows the Western formula "the Spirit who proceeds from the Father *and the Son*," although Pannenberg is also sympathetic with the "Eastern" formula. Wenz concludes, "The unity of Jesus with God is achieved precisely through the strict self-differentiation of Jesus from God."[19]

(iv) Different Spheres of Operation?

All the same, the persons of the Holy Trinity reflect different spheres of operation. The Father, Pannenberg argues, acts in the world only through the Son and Spirit. He himself remains transcendent.[20] Pannenberg asserts, "Through the Son and Spirit, however, the Father, too, stands in relation

17. Moltmann, *The Trinity and the Kingdom of God*, 161–78.

18. Pannenberg, *ST*, vol. 1, 325.

19. Wenz, *Introduction to Wolfhart Pannenberg's Systematic Theology*, 67.

20. Pannenberg, *ST*, vol. 1, 325.

to the history of the economy of salvation. . . . The dependence of the deity of the Father upon the course of events
in the world of creation was first worked out by [Eberhard]
Jüngel [1934–] and then by Moltmann. . . . To speak with
Jüngel, The Father asserts himself against death by raising
up the Crucified. . . . In their intratrinitarian relations the
persons depend on one another in respect of their deity as
well as their personal being."[21]

Pannenberg, finally in this section, alludes to the
well-known theological terms *economic Trinity*, immanent
Trinity, and other such words. The term *economic Trinity* generally denotes God in his "external" relation to the
world. The term *immanent Trinity*, by contrast, generally
denotes God in his "internal" relations between the three
persons of the Trinity. Pannenberg argues that the most
difficult problems arise when we discuss the identity of the
immanent Trinity and the economic Trinity, and we press
each model too far. Cardinal Walter Kasper (1933–2001),
he says, has rightly shown that the equation of the two
signifies a misunderstanding. He concludes, "Only on the
basis of a differentiated concept of the unity of the divine
essence can there finally be also a definition of the Trinitarian persons."[22] God's acts in history concern God as
"economic Trinity."

2. THE "ATTRIBUTES" OR CHARACTER-IN-ACTION OF GOD

We have placed the term *attributes* in quotation marks or in-
verted commas, partly because it is Pannenberg's own chosen word, but chiefly because in current philosophical and
theological discussion the term *attributes* may often reflect

21. Pannenberg, *ST,* vol. 1, 329.
22. Pannenberg, *ST,* vol. 1, 336.

an older Aristotelian approach, which sometimes reflects Aristotle's contrast between substance and attributes. The older systematic theologians Charles Hodge (1797–1878) and A. H. Strong (1836–1921) regularly used this term of God. But Pannenberg insists on a *dynamic* view of the truth of God and the being of God, for which he often uses the word "the contingency of God" and "the contingency of truth." He is keen to avoid any "abstract" understanding of God. This applies both to ontology (God's reality) and to epistemology (how we seek to know God).

Some may find the following section unusually mind-stretching and puzzling. However, in addition to some rather technical discussions of the distinction between God's essence and God's existence, the three things that emerge are the infinite majesty of God, his revelation in terms of action, and his will and his love for the world. This becomes clear if the reader has sufficient patience with the first part of the following discussion.

(i) God's Majesty, Transcendence, and Infinity

Pannenberg begins this section of his *Systematic Theology* by speaking of "the *inconceivable majesty of God which transcends all our concepts*. . . . The lofty mystery that we call God . . . (who is) prior to all our concepts . . . and sustains all being."[23] Since God transcends all human concepts, to attempt to speak of God demands that we consider language about God. Meanwhile, the biblical traditions assure us: "When you seek me with all your heart, I will be found by you" (Jer 29:13–14), and in the Sermon on the Mount "Seek and you will find" (Matt 7:7). They also declare, "No one has ever seen God; the only Son, who is in the bosom of the Father, he has made him known" (John 1:18).

23. Pannenberg, *ST*, vol. 1, 337 (my italics).

Since God indeed has "inconceivable majesty," we must at all costs avoid anthropomorphism. The use of religious language must be critical and accurate, embracing philosophical reflection. Pannenberg speaks further of "the unsearchability of his counsel," "the incomprehensibility of the divine essence," and of the fact that the revelation of God will be completed "only in the eschaton."[24] At the same time we must be aware that God works in world history.

Duns Scotus developed his thesis that the *conceptual* form of human knowledge of God is univocal (i.e., words used of God mean exactly the same thing as words used of created reality). However, Aquinas rightly urged that we can speak only analogically of God (i.e., words used of God do not mean exactly the same thing as words used of created things, contra Scotus, but nor do they mean something utterly different). Pannenberg comments, "We can speak of God only by combining general and distinguishing concepts shaped by the procedure of the older Protestant Dogmatics in its doctrine of God."[25] In other words, even if God's *essence* is incomprehensible, we may still make conceptual statements about God's revealed *acts*. Pannenberg follows Martin Luther, who argued that there is difference between knowing that God exists, and knowing who God is.

Descartes stressed the relevance of the idea of the infinite to the doctrine of God. With the revival of the ontological argument, however, Descartes' grounding of philosophical theology seems to Pannenberg to have reversed the traditional order of the questions *whether* God is, and *what* he is. The idea of God as infinite and perfect must come *first*, and *then* his existence follows from this. This idea is reminiscent of Eberhard Jüngel, he points out, and, we might add, in a very different Anglo-American

24. Pannenberg, *ST*, vol. 1, 340.
25. Pannenberg, *ST*, vol. 1, 346.

tradition, of the Christian philosopher Alvin Plantinga. Pannenberg asserts that God is there, "as the *undefined infinite* which is formed by the primal intuition of our awareness of reality, as the horizon within which we comprehend all else by limitation."[26] He adds, "We can and must think of . . . an existence transcending the world and worldly things only when the essence of God is recognized to be *eternal* and thus *high above the perishability of created beings.*"[27]

(ii) God's Action, the Divine Purpose, and Holiness

Again, Pannenberg insists, "The Son, whose appearing in time anticipates the consummation of the kingdom of God in the world, reveals the eternal Son in relation to whom the Father has from all eternity his existence as Father."[28] In the Bible the divine name revealed in Exodus 3:14 is not a formula revealing the *essence* of God, but a pointer to the experience of his *working in the world* in accordance with his promised action. In line with his earlier comments about God as "economic Trinity" and his action in the world, Pannenberg rightly concludes, "The concept of *divine action* is at the heart of the most significant contributions of modern theology to the doctrine of divine attributes."[29]

In the same vein, Pannenberg quotes Hermann Cremer (1834–1903) as saying that we know God only through his action for us. He discusses God's purposive action according to the New Testament witnesses. This, in turn, brings us to trying to understand *the love of God* as God's will for the world. Pannenberg also discusses the verse in John, "God is Spirit" (John 4:24) alongside Paul's language

26. Pannenberg, *ST,* vol. 1, 356 (my italics).
27. Pannenberg, *ST,* vol. 1, 357 (my italics).
28. Pannenberg, *ST,* vol. 1, 358.
29. Pannenberg, *ST,* vol. 1, 367–68 (my italics).

about the Holy Spirit in 1 Cor 2:11 and 2 Cor 3:17. This, he says, can be linked to the idea of a self-conscious spiritual being as the principle of the divine will. The Spirit of God is a creative life force, and relates especially to God's spirituality and omnipresence. Pannenberg comments, "All things are present to him [God] and are kept by him in his presence. This is not necessarily knowledge in the sense of what is meant by human knowledge and awareness."[30]

It is meaningful to speak of God's *will*, since God has goals of action, though we are clearly speaking in a transferred sense from our understanding of human beings. The concept of a goal presupposes that there is a difference between the object of the will and its fulfillment. God's will may articulate itself as the word of God. The Old Testament has no *single* concept of the will of God. Instead, we have, on the one side, divine commands and ordinances and, on the other, different terms for the divine good pleasure. Pannenberg observed, "In line with biblical ideas, a connection between God's will and Spirit, giving concrete form to the dynamic of the Spirit, leads us to think of a specific orientation of will."[31] Further, he says, "The one God as the living God comes to expression in the living fellowship of Father, Son, and Holy Spirit."[32]

Divine action is important not only from the point of view of the manifestation or invisibility of the acts of God, but also because the three persons of the Trinity become direct subjects of the divine action. God has purposes and a plan, but his plan will be open to all eyes only when God completes his work. Pannenberg writes, "Until then it is hidden from us and talk of it is greeted with derision. . . . Only in the light of the end of history will [its] connections be

30. Pannenberg, *ST,* vol. 1, 380.
31. Pannenberg, *ST,* vol. 1, 382.
32. Pannenberg, *ST,* vol. 1, 383.

fully disclosed. They are thus hidden from us on our way to this end by the inconceivable contingency of the sequence of events which Israel experienced as an expression of the freedom of God in his action."[33] The goal of God's action in the world is twofold: first, the creation of a creaturely reality that is distinct from God and its consolation in encounter with the Creator; second, the revelation of God's deity as the Creator of the world.[34]

By the common action of Father, Son, and Spirit, *the future of God* breaks into the present of his creatures. The futurity of Pannenberg's concept of reality as well as his concept of God is emphasized by numerous interpreters and critics. We select E. Frank Tupper, Stanley Grenz, and Christiaan Mostert as three of many examples.[35] Pannenberg has further comments to make on the divine essence and also on the influence of Hegel. On the former, Grenz comments, "The divine essence can no longer be thought of as a relationless identity transcending the world, but must be seen as inherently rational."[36] On the latter, Grenz argues, "Hegel afforded the doctrine of the Trinity a new central significance for the Christian understanding of God by deriving the Trinity from the concept of God as Spirit. Pannenberg affirms the significance of the Hegelian renewal of an argument that, he points out, was characteristic of Western mediaeval theology as well."[37] Pannenberg argues concerning John's declaration "God is Spirit" (John 4:24)

33. Pannenberg, *ST*, vol. 1, 387 and 388.

34. Pannenberg, *ST*, vol. 1, 389.

35. Tupper, *The Theology of Wolfhart Pannenberg*, 186–230; Grenz, *Reason for Hope*, 11–43, and 188–211; and Mostert, *God and the Future*, throughout.

36. Grenz, *Reason for Hope*, 59.

37. Grenz, *Reason for Hope*, 48.

that it "is one of the few biblical sayings that explicitly characterizes the divine essence as such."[38]

Pannenberg relates the concept of infinity to the concepts of God's holiness, eternity, omnipotence, and omnipresence. *Infinity* stands in contrast to the finite, i.e., to everything limited and transitory. God's *holiness* can threaten the profane world precisely because God does not remain totally otherworldly, but manifests his deity in the human world. God's people stand under the protection of the terrible divine holiness that is a threat to all outside his protective covenant love (Exod 15:11; Isa 10:16). Holiness may take the form of God's "holy zeal."[39] Hosea 11:9, he notes, declares, "I am God and not man, the Holy One in your midst, and I will not come to destroy."

2. FURTHER "ATTRIBUTES" OF GOD

(i) God's Eternity, Omnipresence, and Omnipotence

Pannenberg proceeds to discuss the eternity of God over nine or ten pages. Eternity is not to be thought of simply as unlimited time. Augustine regarded time as a creation of God that was separate from God's eternity. God created the world, he said, *with* time, rather than *in* time. Boethius (480–524) went a step further when he defined eternity as "the simultaneous and perfect presence of unlimited life." Barth rightly applauded this description of eternity as a perfect possession of life.[40] Pannenberg also discusses Nelson Pike's (1930–) *God and Timelessness* (1970), which leaves some important issues out of account. If God is unchangeable, this excludes any possibility of *contingent*

38. Pannenberg, *ST,* vol. 1, 395.

39. Pannenberg, *ST,* vol. 1, 399.

40. Pannenberg, *ST,* vil.1, 404.

action on God's part. God is not to be understood as undifferentiated identity, but as "differentiated unity." But this demands a doctrine of the Trinity.

An important comment now emerges on the difference between eternity and omnipresence. "Whereas God's eternity means that all things are always present *to him*," Pannenberg comments, "the stress on his *omnipresence* is that he is present *to all things* at the place of their existence. God's presence fills heaven and earth (Jer. 23:24)."[41] God's presence transcends all that is made. Even heaven and the heaven of heavens cannot contain him (1 Kgs 8:27). All the same, God's special dwelling is heavenly, rather than located in the realm of the earthly. The Lord's Prayer, for instance, is addressed to "Our Father *in heaven*" (Matt 6:9). But this does not mean that the transcendent God is unable to be present in his creatures by his Spirit. Pannenberg observes, "The doctrine of the Trinity makes it possible to link the transcendence of the Father in heaven with his presence in believers on earth through the Son and Spirit."[42]

Omnipotence and omnipresence are closely related together. God's power is unlimited and infinite, and knows no limits. "Nothing is too hard for you" (Jer 32:17). Pannenberg observes, "As the Creator of all things, God has the right, like the Potter, to throw away imperfect vessels (Isa. 45:9–12; Jer. 18:5–10; Rom. 10:19–21)."[43] Only as the Creator can God be Almighty. Paul describes the God of Abraham in Rom 4:17 as the God "who gives life to the dead and calls into existence the things that do not exist." Moreover, God in his action is not tied for all time to an established order of occurrence. The freedom of the God who acts in history finds expression in the contingency of

41. Pannenberg, *ST*, vol. 1, 410 (his italics).
42. Pannenberg, *ST*, viol.1, 415.
43. Pannenberg, *ST*, vol. 1, 416.

historical events. In the light of what has been said, Pannenberg writes, "We are thus to view the incarnation of the Son as the supreme expression of the omnipotence of God along the lines of the divine will, set already at creation, that the creature should live. . . . It is along the lines of the self-distinction of the Son that by it he distinguishes himself . . . from the deity of the Father and thus moves out of the intratrinitarian life of God."[44]

(ii) God's Self-Giving Love, Dispositional Wrath, and Faithfulness

Pannenberg considers the love of God among the divine "attributes." The well-known passages in John 3:16 and Rom 5:5ff. focus on the fact that *through Jesus* God's love for the world finds expression in the world. The theme of God's love however goes back to Hosea, Jeremiah, and Deuteronomy (Hos 11:1ff., 14:8; Jer 31:3; and Deut 7:8; 10:15). These and other Old Testament passages form the background to those parables that portray God as the one who seeks what is lost, revealing that the divine love takes place through the work and message of Jesus. He notes key biblical passages, such as: the love of God is shed abroad in our hearts (Rom 5:5) and the assertion that "God is love" (1 John 4:8, 16).

In relation to the Holy Trinity, love manifests itself through the reciprocal relation of those who are bound together in love, especially the Father and the Son. In terms of the life in this world, "Each receives his or her self . . . from the other, and since the self-giving is mutual there is no one-sided dependence in the sense of belonging to another."[45] Pannenberg observes further, "The two statements 'God is Spirit' and 'God is love' denote the same unity of essence by which the Father, Son, and Spirit are united in the fellowship

44. Pannenberg, *ST,* vol. 1, 421.
45. Pannenberg, *ST,* vol. 1, 426–27.

of the one God. The statement that God is Spirit tells us what kind of spirit it is whose sound (John 3:8) fills all creation and whose power gives life to all creatures. The Spirit is the power of love that lets the other be."[46]

In underlining the importance that he attaches to the Holy Trinity, Pannenberg repeats what he has earlier said (almost word for word) about the Trinity and about the persons of the Trinity. He writes,

> Each of the three persons is ec-statically related to one or both of the others and has its personal distinctiveness or selfhood in this relation. The Father is the Father only in relation to the Son, in the generation and sending of the Son. The Son is the Son only in obedience to the sending of the Father, which includes recognition of his Fatherhood. The Spirit exists hypostatically as Spirit only as he glorifies the Father in the Son and the Son as sent by the Father.[47]

Combining his consideration of the love of God with his understanding of the Holy Trinity, Pannenberg sees the coming forth of the Son from Father as the basic fulfillment of divine love. Through the creative dynamic of the Spirit, the mutual love between Father, Son, and Spirit becomes apparent. Love becomes apparent in that the persons of the Godhead do not exist for themselves, but in ec-static relation (i.e. without self-centered concern) within the Trinity.

The term "divine love," however, should itself be made more specific. Pannenberg insists that it includes God's goodness (Mark 10:18 and parallels). Paul expounds this goodness in terms of God's grace and favor, which are at work in the history and mission of the Son. This leads

46. Pannenberg, *ST*, vol. 1, 427.

47. Pannenberg, *ST*, vol. 1, 428.

to reconciliation with God the Father (Rom 5:8–11).[48] He also connects God's goodness and righteousness with his faithfulness. Faithfulness expresses the identity and consistency of the eternal God in his loving his creatures. The concept of God's faithfulness is very much more helpful than talk about divine immutability. Pannenberg observes, "In distinction from the idea of immutability, that of God's faithfulness does not exclude historicity or the contingency of world occurrence, nor need the historicity and contingency of the divine action be in contradiction with God's eternity."[49]

On the other hand, Pannenberg declares, "*Wrath* is *not* an attribute of God. His acts are not in general determined by it. In the biblical writings, it is described as a sudden emotional outburst (Num. 11:1; Ps. 2:10–11)."[50] It is understandable that standing outside the British tradition of philosophy, Pannenberg seems unaware of the importance of the term *disposition*. O. R. Jones fully explores this concept to good advantage in his book, *The Concept of Holiness* in 1961. Drawing on Wittgenstein and others, he argues that the wrath of God is a "disposition to behave in a certain way" when particular circumstances arise.[51]

I have attempted to expound the fruitfulness of the concept of disposition in several volumes.[52] At least as important as Wittgenstein on this subject is H. H. Price's (1899–1984) book, *Belief*. Price agrees with Wittgenstein that "Believing . . . is a kind of *disposition* of the believing

48. Pannenberg, *ST*, vol. 1, 433–34.

49. Pannenberg, *ST*, vol. 1, 438.

50. Pannenberg, *ST*, vol. 1, 439 (my italics).

51. Jones, *The Concept of Holiness*, especially 41.

52. Thiselton, Systematic Theology, 43–44 and 370–71; Thiselton, *Approaching the Study of Theology*, 119 and 185–86; Thiselton, *New Horizons in Hermeneutics*, 244.

person. This is shown to me . . . by [someone's] behaviour." "I believe," Price urges, is "equivalent to a series of conditional statements describing what he (the believer) would be likely to say or do or feel if such and such circumstances were to arise."[53] By this means we have no need of such notions as "a sudden emotional outburst."

We are on firmer ground when we consider other ways in which the *love* of God manifests itself. Pannenberg discusses, for example, how patience and wisdom form some of the ways in which God executes world government in his love.[54] Pannenberg writes, "Goodness, grace, mercy, righteousness, faithfulness, patience, and wisdom—are all to be seen as aspects of the comprehensive statement that God is love."[55] Yet all this is definitively revealed only in the future consolation of God's kingdom. The love of God, he says, reaches all creation.

QUESTIONS FOR DISCUSSION

1. How does Pannenberg expound the Fatherhood of God?

2. Is it helpful to approach the doctrine of the Holy Trinity through the Trinitarian "narrative" of the New Testament Gospels?

3. How much careful theological thought is bound up with Pannenberg's notion of God's self-differentiation? Can we suggest similarities with, and differences from, Hegel's notion?

53. Price, *Belief*, 20 (my italics); cf. Wittgenstein, *Philosophical Investigations*, II.x, 191 and Wittgenstein, *Zettel*, sect. 85.

54. Pannenberg, *ST*, vol. 1, 440.

55. Pannenberg, *ST*, vol. 1, 441.

4. What light does Pannenberg shed upon everyday Christian talk about God's will and God's plan? Does he defend these popular terms?

5. How helpful is Pannenberg's understanding of time and eternity? How does he relate time to God's faithfulness?

4

JESUS CHRIST

HIS RESURRECTION, AUTHORITY, UNIQUE ONENESS WITH GOD, AND SAVING WORK

1. THE UNIVERSAL MEANING OF JESUS AND THE RESURRECTION OF JESUS

PANNENBERG INSISTS THAT KNOWLEDGE of God depends on knowledge of Jesus Christ. In *Jesus—God and Man* he writes: "As Christians we know God only as he has been revealed in and through Jesus. All other talk about God can have, at most, provisional significance."[1] As we have already noted in our Introduction, Pannenberg attacked the inadequacy of Martin Kähler's emphasis on "signifi-cance" in preaching and subjective experience, as well as Rudolf Bultmann's interpretation of Jesus, which also ends

1. Pannenberg, *JGM*, 19.

in subjective, existential experience. In contrast to them, he remains concerned with genuine historical events that occurred at *a particular time and place.*

Pannenberg, however, is also concerned to stress the universal meaning of Jesus, and his authoritative status as one whom God raised at his resurrection, and to focus on Jesus Christ as the raised and exalted Lord. To quote Pannenberg again: "Only on the basis of what happened in the past, not because of the present experiences, do we know that Jesus lives as the exalted Lord. Only in trust in the reliability of the report of Jesus' resurrection and exaltation are we able to turn in prayer to the one always exalted and who now lives."[2] Further, he comments, "Therefore, theology and Christology, the doctrine of God and the doctrine of Jesus as the Christ, are bound together. It is the goal of theology as well as of Christology to develop this connection. . . . The procedure of Christology . . . begins with Jesus himself in order to find God in him."[3] In his *Systematic Theology* he commented, "We can know even God himself only in that which took place here below, in the human history of Jesus of Nazareth."[4]

In this chapter, I shall primarily follow the sequence and argument of *Jesus—God and Man*, but also cite arguments and comments from Pannenberg's later thoughts in his *Systematic Theology*, as well as from other works.

(i) The Method of Christology

Pannenberg believes that notions of pre-existence, of incarnation, and of Trinity do not stand at the *beginning* of Christological development. Dogmatics may not presuppose the

2. Pannenberg, *JGM,* 28.
3. Pannenberg, *JGM,* 20.
4. Pannenberg, *ST*, vol. 2, 281.

historical result of this development. But he continues to ask: how else is the history of Jesus supposed to substantiate faith in him except by showing itself to be the revelation of God?[5] This invites one of his regular comments: "Jesus' own message . . . can only be understood within the *horizon of apocalyptic expectations*"; to which he adds, "The God whom Jesus called 'Father' was none other than the God of the Old Testament."[6]

In considering the *method* of Christology, Pannenberg contrasts what he describes as Christology "from below" with Christology "from above." He considers the method of Christology also later in his *Systematic Theology*, in which he scarcely departs from his conclusions in *Jesus—God and Man*.[7] In the latter, he expresses his concern to take into account "the total character of the coming of Jesus," and not only that of the earthly Jesus.[8] A Christology from below first considers the historical man Jesus of Nazareth and then rises to recognize his divinity and his resurrection, as the culmination of the concept of the incarnation. This method is followed by Matthew at the beginning of his Gospel, by introducing Jesus first as descended from David. On the other hand, Christology from above begins, as John's Gospel begins, with Jesus as the Logos, the Word of God, and then seeks to illuminate how the divine Logos took on humanity. This method was far more common in the ancient church, from Ignatius of Antioch and the second-century Apologists to the Alexandrian theologians of the fourth century, including especially Athanasius, and in the fifth century, especially Cyril of Alexandria (378–444).

5. Pannenberg *JGM,* 30.
6. Pannenberg, *JGM,* 32.
7. Pannenberg, *ST,* vol. 2, 278–97.
8. Pannenberg, *ST,* vol. 2, 280.

Pannenberg admits that the New Testament contains isolated examples of the latter Christology: especially in Phil 2:5–11; Rom 8:3; and Gal 4:4. In modern theology the approach of Karl Barth characteristically adopts the approach of Christology from above. Pannenberg himself, by contrast, insists that we must *begin* with a Christology *from below*, namely with the historical reality of Jesus of Nazareth. Nevertheless, he writes, "While Christology must begin with the man Jesus, its first question has to be about his unity with God. Every statement about Jesus taken independently from his relationship to God could result [only] in a crass distortion of his historical reality."[9] Martin Luther was successful in adopting this dual approach. There is nothing irrational in adopting this approach.

(ii) The Resurrection of Jesus Christ

Many historical investigations of Christology rightly tie this subject closely with an understanding of Christ as the bringer of salvation. Anselm of Canterbury provided such an example in his book *Why God Became Man*. This emphasizes a Christology of God's grace alone, while Jesus remains the representative of all people before God. Pannenberg admits the dangers of projecting a later Christology onto Jesus, but argues that this should not necessarily be the case. He issued the warning, "The establishment of the universal significance of Jesus, which is derived from God, cannot be replaced by talking about the fulfilment of the humanity of man through Jesus. Otherwise both the universality of Jesus and his saving significance for us become mere assertions [of belief]."[10]

9. Pannenberg, *JGM,* 36.
10. Pannenberg, *JGM,* 49.

In chapter 3 of *Jesus—God and Man*, Pannenberg discusses the resurrection of Jesus as *the ground for our belief in his unity with God* and his unique claim to authority. Numerous modern theologians have tried to locate the authority of Jesus in his pre-Easter life and work, including Albrecht Ritschl, Wilhelm Herrmann (1846–1922), Friedrich Gogarten, Ernst Käsemann (1906–98), and Günther Bornkamm (1905–90). Pannenberg, however, acknowledges the importance of his resurrection and the apostolic proclamation of this as "constitutive" for his authority and identity.[11] Thus, by contrast, "If Jesus has been raised, then the end of the world has begun. The universal resurrection of the dead and the judgement are imminent."[12] Jesus is the firstborn among many brothers (Rom 8:29); Christ is raised as the firstfruits of those who are falling asleep (1 Cor 15:20); Jesus is the firstborn of the dead (Col 1:18). The same Holy Spirit who raised Jesus Christ from the dead also dwells in Christian believers, and brings them into the new creation (Rom 8:11).

Pannenberg explains, "If Jesus has been raised, this can only mean that God himself has confirmed the pre-Easter activity of Jesus. Jesus' claim to authority, through which he has put himself in God's place, was blasphemous for Jewish ears."[13] He writes further: "If Jesus, having been raised from the dead, is ascended to God, and if thereby the end of the world has begun, then God is ultimately revealed in Jesus. Only at the end of all events can God be revealed in his divinity, that is, as the one who works all things, who has power over everything. . . . Only because the end of the world is already present in Jesus'

---

11. Pannenberg, *ST,* vol. 2, 288.

12. Pannenberg, *JGM,* 66.

13. Pannenberg, *JGM,* 67.

resurrection is God himself revealed in him."[14] He concludes, "Material primacy belongs to the eternal Son, who
has become man by his incarnation."[15]

Pannenberg admits that the apocalyptic frame of reference would be relevant primarily to Jewish readers, but
argues that the concept of the *Logos* (the Word) and of the
Son would be a comparable concept for Hellenistic and
gentile readers. At the same time, he argues, the eschatological resurrection of Jesus as resurrection of the Crucified
One would soon become intelligible in the gentile mission.
The gentile mission, he argues, is bound up with the proclamation of the Lordship of Jesus Christ in heaven, and the
news of his Lordship would be carried to all nations.[16] In
commenting on the words of the risen Jesus, once again he
characteristically insists, "*Word and event belong together* in
the appearances of the resurrection of Jesus."[17]

The concept of the resurrection, both of Jesus and of
the general resurrection of the dead, is by no means self-
evident in meaning. Hence, following Paul, Pannenberg
appeals to the analogy of being awakened from sleep in
everyday life. He writes, "The familiar experience of being
awakened and rising from sleep serves as a parallel for the
completely unknown destiny expected for the dead."[18]

Pannenberg uses exactly the same metaphor of being
awakened from sleep in his *Systematic Theology*. He writes,
"When we waken from sleep we 'rise' up. So it is with the
dead. Underlying this metaphoric usage is the further metaphor that was common in both Jewish and Greek thinking,

---

14. Pannenberg, *JGM,* 68–69.

15. Pannenberg, *ST,* vol. 2, 289.

16. Pannenberg, *JGM,* 71.

17. Pannenberg, *JGM,* 72 (my italics).

18. Pannenberg, *JGM,* 74.

namely the idea of death as a sleep."[19] The raising from the dead is to a new and eternal life. He appeals here to biblical evidence for resurrection in Isa 26:19 ("Your dead shall live, their bodies shall arise") and Dan 12:2; as well as to the books of the Pseudepigrapha, Ethiopian Enoch 92:3, and the Syriac Apocalypse of Baruch 30:1.

In the New Testament Paul speaks of resurrection in 1 Thess 4:13–17, and in 1 Cor 11:30; 15:6, 20, 51. The only possible way of speaking of the resurrection of believers is metaphorical.[20] Here he reaffirms the point that resurrection is experienced "not as the mere resuscitation of a corpse, but as radical transformation."[21] It will *not* be like the raising of Lazarus, or the daughter of Jairus, which was indeed resuscitation to continue life in the body. Pannenberg concludes that the basis of the knowledge of Jesus and his significance remains bound to the original apocalyptic horizon of Jesus' history.[22]

Pannenberg now continues his exposition under the title "Resurrection as a Historical Problem." He fully recognizes the regular scholarly opinions about the two traditions often described as the appearances tradition and the empty-tomb tradition. He asserts, "Mark still offers an unadulterated account of the empty tomb."[23] In his view it is significant that while Paul focuses on the appearances of the resurrected Lord, 1 Corinthians reports the appearance of the resurrected Christ to Peter, to the twelve, and to five hundred Christian brethren at once, then to James, then to all the apostles, and finally to Paul himself. Pannenberg comments, "The intention of this enumeration is clearly to

19. Pannenberg, *ST*, vol. 2, 346.

20. Pannenberg, *JGM*, 75.

21. Pannenberg, *JGM*, 76.

22. Pannenberg, *JGM*, 83.

23. Pannenberg, *JGM*, 88.

give proof by means of witnesses to the *facticity* of Jesus' resurrection."[24] He wrote, "The appearance to 500 brethren at once cannot be a secondary construction to be explained by the development of the history of traditions, because Paul calls attention precisely here to the possibility of checking his assertion by saying that most of the 500 are still alive."[25] In his *Systematic Theology* he once again considers carefully the relationship between the "empty tomb" tradition and the "appearances" tradition.[26] He rightly concludes, "The report of the resurrection implied that *the tomb was empty*."[27] Again, he repeats as his own verdict what he quoted earlier from Paul Althaus (1888–1966), "*The first Christians could not have successfully preached the resurrection of Jesus if his body had been intact in the tomb.*"[28]

Pannenberg refers here not only to Walter Künneth (1901–97), but quotes with approval the words of Althaus: the kerygma (the gospel proclamation) "could not have been maintained in Jerusalem for a single day, for a single hour, if the emptiness of the tomb had not been established as a fact for all concerned."[29] In his *Systematic Theology* he comments, "Without the resurrection the apostles would have no missionary message. . . . Without this event, as Paul wrote to the Corinthians (1 Cor. 15:17), the faith of Christians is vain. . . . The Easter event means directly that God himself justified the condemned and executed Jesus, namely by the Spirit, by whose power he was raised from the dead."[30] Pannenberg adds that in this way God con-

24. Pannenberg, *JGM*, 89. (Italics mine.)

25. Pannenberg, *JGM*, 97.

26. Pannenberg, *ST*, vol. 2, 349–63.

27. Pannenberg, *ST*, vol. 2, 357 (my italics).

28. Pannenberg, *ST*, vol. 2, 358 (my italics).

29. Pannenberg, *JGM*, 100.

30. Pannenberg, *ST*, vol. 2, 344.

firmed the claim that was implicit in the work of Jesus, i.e., that the imminent rule of God that Jesus proclaimed was about to break in and in fact was already doing so for those who trusted his message. He concludes, "The Easter event certainly shed a new light on the death of Jesus, on his earthly ministry, and therefore on his person."[31]

Since the resurrection of Jesus is so central to his thought, Pannenberg is rightly concerned to address the long-standing problem of the delay of the *parousia*, the final return of Christ. He concedes that the earliest apostles may have thought that the interval between the resurrection of Jesus and the End would not be huge. Nevertheless, he insists, "The question as to how much time might elapse between the appearance of Jesus and the coming of the Son of Man is completely irrelevant. . . . Neither the two-thousand-year interval from the time of Jesus' birth appearance nor its quantitative growth is sufficient in itself to let the connection between the activity . . . of Jesus and the expected End of all things become untenable. . . . The delay of the End-events . . . is not a refutation of the Christian hope."[32] The delay of the final coming of Christ never became a major problem in the eyes of the early Christian church.

2. THE MODE OF GOD'S PRESENCE IN JESUS: HIS UNITY WITH GOD

(i) Jesus as Lord, Logos, and Son of God

In chapter 4 of *Jesus—God and Man*, Pannenberg discusses the divinity of Jesus in relation to the divinity of God the Father, and Jesus' unity with God. He discusses Gal 4:4

31. Pannenberg, *ST*, vol. 2, 345.
32. Pannenberg, *JGM*, 107–8.

and especially Rom 1:3–4, where Paul presupposed the pre-existence of Christ, and drew a contrast between Jesus "according to the flesh" and Jesus "according to the Spirit." He connects this "double assessment of Jesus" with other verses, which include 1 Tim 3:16 and 1 Pet 3:18. The phrase "according to the Spirit" immediately invokes a reference to the Holy Spirit, through whom the essential presence of God in Jesus is mediated. In Pannenberg's judgment, this points to the self-revelation of God. The Christ event is God's revelation, as when Paul refers to the appearance of the glory of God in the face of Jesus Christ (2 Cor 4:6). The concept of God's *self*-revelation contains the idea that the Revealer and what is revealed are identical. In an important sentence Pannenberg writes, "The essence of God is not accessible at all without Jesus Christ."[33] God is essentially the God who gives life to the dead, as God demonstrated in the resurrection of Jesus Christ.

Paul and those who addressed the Hellenistic church constantly used the word "Lord" as well as naming him the eschatological Son of God. Pannenberg asks the question: are the virgin birth and the concept of Jesus' pre-existence contradictory? Pannenberg sees a contradiction between Jesus' *becoming* "God's Son through Mary's conception" and Paul and John's witness that "the Son of God was already preexistent and then as a preexistent being had bound himself to the man Jesus."[34] With the biblical writers, *we must retain an emphasis on the initiative of God,* but also with the continuity between nature and the man Jesus. As a faithful Lutheran, Pannenberg rejects the path of Roman Mariology and Mariological speculation. On the virgin birth, he said, "Gynocology is not the issue, but pneumatology."[35]

33. Pannenberg, *JGM,* 130.
34. Pannenberg, *JGM,* 143.
35. Pannenberg, *ST,* vol. 2, 318.

The Gospel of John adopts a parallel approach in the doctrine of the *Logos,* who became flesh, or took upon himself ordinary human existence. In his *Systematic Theology,* he urges, "Because we are alienated from the Logos, we learn to know the *Logos*—who is still the origin of life and the light of our consciousness—only through Jesus."[36] Because the *Logos,* or the Word, according to John, *was God,* Pannenberg asserts, "It is quite legitimate to speak of *God's having become man.*"[37] Further, Jesus as *person* cannot be separated from God's essence. . . . Jesus understood himself as set over against God whom he called Father. He distinguishes the Father from himself."[38] Pannenberg concludes this subsection with the comment, "The deity of Jesus Christ cannot therefore have the sense of undifferentiated identity with the divine nature. . . . This was the opinion of modalism concerning Jesus' divinity."[39] He adds, "The merit of the so-called Logos Christology . . . is that it asserted the differentiation of the Father and Son within the Godhead."[40]

(ii) God's Self-Differentiation: The Spirit, Hegel, and the Father

In agreement with Moltmann, Pannenberg comments that the Spirit is the Spirit of *life.* The Spirit is life-creating. He regularly appeals to biblical passages which regard the Holy Spirit as the one who raised Christ from the dead, and who will give life to our mortal bodies (Rom 8:11; 2 Cor 1:22). Like Moltmann, he regrets that too much contemporary theology lacks the doctrine of the Holy Spirit that

36. Pannenberg, *ST,* vol. 2, 295.
37. Pannenberg, *JGM,* 156 (my italics).
38. Pannenberg, *JGM,* 158.
39. Pannenberg, *JGM,* 159.
40. Pannenberg, *JGM,* 160.

corresponds in breadth and specificity to the biblical concept of the Spirit.[41] Rightly Pannenberg comments, "The Spirit guarantees the participation of believers in the living Jesus Christ."[42] He helpfully refers to further biblical passages and to the work of Basil of Caesarea.

When he considers the unity of the Trinity, Pannenberg makes an extremely important statement: "*The Father is Father only vis-à-vis the Son; the Son is Son only vis-à-vis the Father; the Spirit is Spirit only as the bond of the community* [i.e. intimate relationship] *of Father and Son.* No one of the Trinitarian persons is who he is without the others; each exists only in reference to the others."[43] Pannenberg rightly and convincingly points out that before the mediaeval era few, if any, had understood that the word "person" was an *inter*-personal term. It was hardly applicable to an *isolated individual*. However, Richard of Victor (1110–1173) in the twelfth century pointed a way forward by defining the very concept of "person" as entailing a relation.

In spite of those critics who trace the notion of the *self-differentiation of God* to Hegel, Pannenberg shows convincingly how Hegel's philosophy (as well as Scripture) becomes a beginning point for better understanding the doctrine of the Holy Trinity.

In his *Philosophy of Religion,* Hegel was the first to elaborate the concept of "person" in such a way that God's unity became understandable precisely from the *reciprocity* of the divine persons. Pannenberg says explicitly: "The God who reveals himself is essentially person."[44] Here he clearly stands in contrast to Barth, who rejects the notion of "person" in favor of "mode of being" when speaking of God.

41. Pannenberg, *JGM,* 171.
42. Pannenberg, *JGM,* 172.
43. Pannenberg, *JGM,* 181 (my italics).
44. Pannenberg, *JGM,* 182.

In this part of the discussion Pannenberg refers to Hegel. Hegel, he says, understood the unity of the Trinity as the "unity of self-dedication," which allowed "the sharpest accentuation of the concept of the personality of Father, Son, and Spirit."[45] Pannenberg argued: "The relation of Jesus to the Father is entirely characterised by the dedication of the Son to the Father, that of the Father to Jesus by his acknowledgement of the Son in his raising Jesus from the dead. The Holy Spirit moves the believer to dedication to Jesus through believing trust and through praise."[46] He emphasizes the doxological and proleptic character of this Trinitarian action, which reflects the influence of Edmund Schlink (1903–84).[47]

3. JESUS CHRIST AS REPRESENTATIVE MAN, AND HIS SAVING WORK

In his next main Part, Pannenberg suggested the title, "Jesus the Man before God." He argued that Jesus was and is historically unique, not only in his genuine humanness, but also *in his relation to God*. Jesus is the representative of humankind before God. Jesus has become the fulfillment of the human destiny of communion, or intimate relationship, with God.[48] What we can say about his divinity can be seen only by looking backward from his resurrection. Through the resurrection Christ has become legitimated by God as the new Adam.

---

45. Hegel, *Lectures on the Philosophy of Religion*, vol. 3, 24–25.

46. Pannenberg, *JGM*, 183.

47. Schlink, *The Coming Christ and the Coming Church*, 96–118.

48. Pannenberg, *JGM*, 196.

(i) Jesus Christ as Obedient Servant of God, and the Last Adam

Jesus' life has become well-pleasing in the eyes of God, notably in his dedication to his duly appointed role and acceptance of his fate at Calvary. Paul, Pannenberg asserts, described Jesus Christ as the eschatological form of humanity that in contrast to the previous Adamic humanity, obeys God, and overcomes mortality. He continues in his *Systematic Theology*, "Such a description, like John's view of Jesus as the incarnate *Logos*, expresses the claim of a universal relevance for Jesus' person and history that goes far beyond the sphere of Jewish faith."[49] Timothy Bradshaw comments, "Jesus' Sonship . . . fulfils human personality by virtue of his total openness and trust."[50]

In his *Systematic Theology,* Pannenberg majors on the notion of the *universal significance* of Jesus as the *last Adam*. He writes, "Paul's view of Jesus Christ as the new eschatological or a last Adam has a social reference orientated to human community. It tells us that 'we' who shall bear the image of the new and heavenly man (1 Cor. 15:49) shall be changed into his likeness (2 Cor. 3:18)."[51] We shall all be changed into the likeness of Jesus Christ. He comments, "Jesus Christ is the paradigm of all humanity in its relation to God. Yet as in the case of the new Adam, he is our representative, not as we now are but as we are to be."[52]

---

49. Pannenberg, *ST,* vol. 2, 297.

50. Bradshaw, *Pannenberg,* 101.

51. Pannenberg, *ST,* vol. 2, 304.

52. Pannenberg, *ST,* vol. 2, 430.

(ii) The Three Offices of Jesus Christ, and Human Alienation from God

Whatever his criticisms of Schleiermacher, Pannenberg approves of his notion that the Redeemer founded a new human fellowship in God's kingdom, that is, freed from the dominion of sin.[53] He writes, "By depicting Jesus as the new eschatological Adam, and therefore as the definitive form of humanity, the apostle Paul has given expression to the universal significance of the person and history of Jesus in the light of the Easter event—a significance that reaches far beyond the people of Israel."[54]

Pannenberg notes that the three traditional offices that are ascribed to Jesus Christ, as Prophet, Priest, and King, were first formulated by Andreas Osiander in 1530, and endorsed by John Calvin in 1536. Their main argument was that prophets, priests, and kings were *anointed* for their office and work, and that Jesus was pre-eminently the Anointed One. Pannenberg, perhaps surprisingly, rejects the formal notion of three offices. He argues that the title "Prophet" depends on the teaching activity of Jesus, and that his teaching was primary a call to repentance and announcement of the kingdom of God. He also argued that the office of "King" cannot be primary, at least before the resurrection. He is only *potentially* King.[55] Jesus proclaimed essentially the Kingship and the Lordship of *God*, which would begin in his own generation (Matt 23:36; Mark 13:30; and parallels). The coming of salvation could be seen in the *nearness of the kingdom of God.*

53. Pannenberg, *ST*, vol. 2, 308.
54. Pannenberg, *ST*, vol. 2, 315.
55. Pannenberg, *JGM*, 216–18.

In his central message, Jesus proclaims not only the nearness of God's kingdom.[56] He also proclaimed *the Fatherhood of God*. In a general sense, he admitted, Israel thought of God as Father. But Jesus uses the term with *unique intimacy*, and he insists on his Fatherly care of all creation (Matt 10:29–30). Again, he insists that the two-thousand-year interval today after Jesus' proclamation of the imminent arrival of the kingdom does not militate against the fulfillment of Jesus' teaching in his own resurrection. He explains, "We experience this continuity as long as we retain the expectation and hope for its universal consequence that has not happened yet, namely the universal resurrection of the dead as entrance into the kingdom of God."[57] Again, he asserted that the dying out of the first generation of believers did not result in the shaking of the Christian faith.

(iii) Vicarious Substitution and the Divine "Must": The Necessity of God's Purpose

In chapter 7 of *Jesus—God and Man*, Pannenberg expounds the meaning of Jesus' vicarious death on the cross. He wrote, "*Jesus's death on the cross is revealed in the light of his resurrection as the punishment suffered in our place for the blasphemous existence of humanity.*"[58] In commenting on the oldest interpretations of the death of Jesus, he insists that the divine "*must*" stood over Jesus' passion according to Mark 8:31; 14:24, 49; Luke 22:20; and other biblical passages. He discusses the *universality of human sin* further in his *Systematic Theology*.[59] We shall return to this subject later.

56. Pannenberg, *Theology and the Kingdom of God*, 51–56.

57. Pannenberg, *JGM*, 242.

58. Pannenberg, *JGM*, 245 (my italics).

59. Pannenberg, *ST*, vol. 2, 175–276.

Meanwhile he writes, "As the Messiah, he does not exercise dominion through political power, but, through vicarious suffering for human sins, Jesus not only changed Jewish hope . . . but also opened it up with a view to the reconciliation of the Gentile world with Israel and its God."[60]

Similarly, in his *Systematic Theology*, Pannenberg writes, "Nothing unforeseen or unplanned can happen to the Son of God. Only on the side of his human nature may we distinguish between his active coming and work on the one side and the fate that he suffers on the other."[61] Further, "As the self-offering of the Son for the reconciliation of the world and his being offered up by the Father are one and the same event and form a single process, so we are to see the work of the exhorted Christ and that of the Spirit."[62]

Once again, Pannenberg constantly emphasizes the importance of the *divine purpose and decree*, which he had examined in his doctoral and post-graduate thesis. The cross lies ahead by divine necessity. The earliest biblical passages use the figure of ransom, which was probably taken from Isa 53:10. Paul, he argued, saw this in terms of taking upon himself the curse of the law, as in Gal 3:30. Yet again he emphasizes that the resurrection of Jesus must be understood entirely as the act of God, which vindicated and confirmed all the previous life and teaching of Jesus.

Pannenberg endorsed the notion of the death of Jesus as *substitution*. He saw this theme as arising from both the Lord's Supper tradition (Luke 22:27) and from the sayings about ransom (Mark 10:45).[63] The resurrection reveals

60. Pannenberg, *ST,* vol. 2, 315.

61. Pannenberg, *ST,* vol. 2, 443.

62. Pannenberg, *ST,* vol. 2, 450.

63. Cf. Pannenberg, *ST,* vol. 2, 417. Cf. Pannenberg, *ST,* vol. 2, 419, and 416–37, which also draws Paul's Lord's Supper tradition from 1 Cor 11 into the discussion.

that Jesus died as a righteous man, not as a sinner or blasphemer. Pannenberg continues, "Jesus' death has vicarious significance for all humanity."[64] He argued that the Enlightenment criticism of substitution began because of their *individualistic concept of guilt and responsibility*. We cannot reject substitution on this basis.[65]

(iv) Separation from God as Implying Penal Substitution

It is perhaps important to quote Pannenberg's own words on the issue of penal substitution. He wrote:

> God himself, who raised Jesus, had laid on him the punishment. . . . *In his death Jesus bore the consequences of separation from God, the punishment for sin, not just in place of his people, but in place of all humanity*. Through him, however, the God-forsakenness of death is overcome for all men. No longer must anyone die alone and without hope.[66]

In his *Systematic Theology*, Pannenberg makes a fundamentally crucial statement about terminology and vocabulary. He writes, "The fact that a later age may find it hard to understand traditional ideas is not a sufficient reason for replacing them. It simply shows how necessary it is to open up these ideas to later generations by interpretation, and thus to keep their meaning alive." He cites as examples "ideas like expiation and representation (or substitution) in our secularized age."[67] The blame for misunderstanding, he

64. Pannenberg, *JGM*, 261.
65. Pannenberg, *JGM*, 267–68.
66. Pannenberg, *JGM*, 269 (my italics).
67. Pannenberg, *ST*, vol. 2, 422.

says, does not lie with the terms, but with failures to explain the terms with sufficient forcefulness.

Some might take exception to Pannenberg's universal emphasis. But the universality of the death of Jesus remains an important part of his general argument. He discusses the *symbolic* meaning of the death of Jesus as a ransom for sin and the devil. We might be tempted to imagine that the term "symbolic" weakens the force of the notion of ransom. But Pannenberg has a stronger reason for this. He wrote, "Because the expressions have only symbolic character, the question of *to whom* the ransom was paid does not arise."[68] He pointed out that Anselm of Canterbury was one who expressly rejected the misapplication of this term.

Pannenberg carefully examines Anselm's Satisfaction Theory. He thoroughly approves of Anselm's "must" (i.e,. the divine *necessity*) of the divine plan, but considers that Luther's ideas came closer to the meaning of the cross itself, because of his emphasis on God, rather than on man. Luther emphasizes that the event of the cross is an action of *God*, even if in and through Jesus. Discussing Paul's formulations of the atonement in Gal 3:13; 2 Cor 5:21; and Rom 6:3, he finds in these a regular reference to *vicarious penal suffering*.[69] In his *Systematic Theology* he writes, "Vicarious penal suffering, which is rightly described as the vicarious suffering of the wrath of God at sin, rests on the fellowship that Jesus Christ accepted with all of us as sinners and with our fate as such."[70]

Pannenberg concludes, "What is at issue is the way to the salvation of the world through overcoming the opposition to God into which sin and death have plunged us. . . .

---

68. Pannenberg, *JGM*, 275 (my italics).

69. Pannenberg, *JGM*, 279.

70. Pannenberg, *ST*, vol. 2, 427.

God's act in reconciling the world certainly took place in Christ's passion."[71] Jesus is our "Savior" (Phil 3:20).

4. THE DIVINITY OF JESUS AND THE CONTROVERSY ABOUT "TWO NATURES" CHRISTOLOGY

(i) Complications and Complexities in Historical Developments in Christology

At this point, Pannenberg began the final Part of his book *Jesus—God and Man* by discussing the divinity of Christ and the human Jesus. He helpfully insists that whether we begin with the divinity of Jesus or his humanity, we begin with the same person. The problem with a "two natures" Christology is an insoluble problem, as if to suggest two opposed substances. Pannenberg is so concerned about this problem that he uses the two terms "unification Christology" and "disjunction Christology" to denote each.[72] The Antiochene theologians, he remarks, left unexplained how man and God would be united in one person, because in practice their's constituted a "disjunction" Christology. In the wake of this, "dyothelitism" (the notion Jesus Christ having "two wills") became the dogma of the church. A more sophisticated and adequate answer comes with the notion of the *mutual interpenetration of the two natures* of Christ.[73] Pannenberg notes that the notion of a mutual interpenetration (*perichōrēsis*) was mentioned by Gregory of Nazianzus (329–90).

71. Pannenberg, *ST,* vol. 2, 437.

72. Pannenberg, *JGM,* 287–95.

73. Pannenberg devoted a section of his discussion to this in his *Systematic Theology* (*ST,* vol. 2, 379–89). But his conclusion there broadly remains that of *Jesus—God and Man.*

The Cappadocian Fathers did attempt to combine the unity of Christ's person with the notion of a simultaneous distinction between them. They argued that the divinity of Christ "saturated" Jesus' humanity, as fire makes iron glow, while the humanity of Jesus dissolved itself in his divinity, as a drop of vinegar dissolves in an infinite sea. In modern thought, Hegel and Rahner tried to formulate this dialectic. We must retain the unity of Jesus Christ, Pannenberg argues, and we must give due attention to this genuine divinity and humanity. At the same time we need to understand genuine uniqueness of Jesus as a revelation of God himself. Luther's approach was to attempt a solution in terms of *kenōsis* (self-emptying), as in Phil 2:7–11.

(ii) Divinity and Self-Limitation: Christ's Relation to God the Father

Pannenberg's penultimate chapter in *Jesus—God and Man* focuses on Jesus' personal unity with God. He urges that a self-limitation of the divinity of Christ at the incarnation results (negatively) in a transformation of the Trinity. God cannot cease to be God. But how can God and man be united in Christ with a *continuing differentiation between the two*?[74] Some theologians rejected the notion of the *kenōsis* (self-emptying) of the *Logos*, because of God's unchangeable reality. But Jesus Christ was and is unique. Pannenberg insists, "One must unavoidably distinguish between *Jesus' eternal Sonship* [which does not change] *and his human being that began at a particular point in time*."[75]

The Gospel of John is a special witness to this unity with God. John recounts not only the "I am" sayings of Jesus, but also the statement "I and the Father are one" (John

74. Pannenberg, *JGM,* 311–14.
75. Pannenberg, *JGM,* 325 (my italics).

10:30). The unity of Jesus with God, Pannenberg comments, manifests itself in the activity, as well as the speech, of Jesus, both of which were on God's own authority. Most of all, this became demonstrated in the *utter trust* of Jesus in God at the cross. We see here the utter dedication to God and his will that characterized the life of Jesus. But we also see the true divinity of the Son and his relationship to the Father, in a Trinitarian framework. In his *Systematic Theology* he writes, "This uniqueness of Jesus rested on the unconditional subordination of his person to the Lordship of God that he proclaimed."[76] This included that "In truth he suffered in our place as sinners."[77]

Pannenberg paid special attention to Jesus' Sonship as the fulfillment of human personality and destiny. He wrote, "Precisely in his Sonship, in his relation to the Father, all others shall receive a share through him. God has sent his Son that we might receive sonship through him."[78] Through the Spirit of sonship, he urged, "the Son of God wants to become person-building, existence-integrating power in all men."[79]

In his *Systematic Theology* he continued and developed these thoughts. He wrote, "The filial relationship of Jesus to the Father is the basic form of our human destiny of fellowship with God. . . . Only in Jesus Christ has the basic filial relationship, for which we are destined, come to full and definitive manifestation."[80] He also argues, "The idea of the sending of the Son presupposes his pre-existence, his being in the eternity of God in correspondence with the eternity of the Father."[81]

76. Pannenberg, *ST,* vol. 2, 373.

77. Pannenberg, *ST,* vol. 2, 374.

78. Pannenberg, *JGM,* 345.

79. Pannenberg, *JGM,* 346.

80. Pannenberg, *ST,* vol. 2, 317.

81. Pannenberg, *ST,* vol. 2, 316.

Pannenberg next considers the freedom of Jesus and his holiness. The latter especially means Jesus' vicarious substitution for us. He wrote, "Jesus was judged, cursed, treated as a sinner, by God in our stead. Only because Jesus was himself without sin can it be said that what he suffered was not a consequence of his own guilt, but that he took his suffering upon himself for our sake."[82] Pannenberg also remarks that an understanding of the sinlessness of Jesus merely as irreproachable moral behavior presupposes an all-too-superficial concept of sin.[83]

The holiness of Jesus, his self-sacrifice, and self-emptying genuinely reflects the character of God. Pannenberg wrote, "The self-emptying and self-humbling that we find when we compare the eternal deity of the Son to his incarnation must not be seen as a limitation, but as *an expression of the eternal deity*. . . . The eternal self-distinction from the Father contains already the elements of self-emptying."[84]

5. THE LORDSHIP OF JESUS CHRIST

In the final chapter of *Jesus—God and Man*, Pannenberg considers the Lordship of Jesus Christ, including his Kingship, the summation of history in Christ ,and the creation of the world through Jesus Christ. He wrote, "The participation of the man Jesus in the omnipotent Lordship of God over his creation is the crowning aspect of the unity of God established in the unity of God and man in Jesus Christ."[85] This was properly achieved in his resurrection from the dead, which also showed divine approval of the earthly life and work of Jesus.

82. Pannenberg, *JGM*, 355.
83. Pannenberg, *JGM*, 361.
84. Pannenberg, *ST*, vol. 2, 320 (my italics).
85. Pannenberg, *JGM*, 365.

(i) The Pre-Easter Jesus

Pannenberg insisted that the pre-Easter Jesus did not proclaim *his own* Lordship, but the coming kingly rule *of God*. The Lordship of Christ is part of *his exaltation*, as stated by Phil 2:11, as well as his explicit Sonship of God. This is implied by Rom 1:4. Through the resurrection, the Revealer of God's eschatological will became the incarnation of the eschatological reality itself. Pannenberg concludes, "If the Son rules, he rules as the Son, and that means he rules in dedication to the Father and his Lordship."[86] In his *Systematic Theology*, Pannenberg writes, "The fundamental thought was that those who open themselves to the summons of God's rule, who accept its imminence and thus receive present salvation, must also let themselves be drawn into the movement of the love of God as it aims beyond individual recipients to the world as a whole."[87]

As God's Son, Jesus brings the entire creation into the obedience of sonship, thereby mediating it into immediacy to the Father. The Book of Revelation, Pannenberg urges, speaks of the Lordship and throne of the Lamb. The coming Lordship of Christ established the kingdom of the Father, even though it is partly hidden on earth today. Pannenberg concludes, "In summary, it may be said that the exalted Lord already rules in his church (as also in the world) and is recognised by Christians (in distinction from the world) as ruler, but that the full participation of Christians in the Kingdom of Christ still belongs to the future. The Lordship of Christ in his church, as Luther said, occurs through the Word of the gospel."[88] The kingdom of God cannot be identified with some present political order.

86. Pannenberg, *JGM*, 369.

87. Pannenberg, *ST*, vol. 2, 332.

88. Pannenberg, *JGM*, 372.

When he turns to consider the summation of humanity in Jesus Christ, Pannenberg reintroduces his regular theme of *divine necessity in the crucifixion of Christ*. He understands that both Matthew and Luke, in their concern for the fulfillment of particular words of Scripture, are commenting on a theology of history in the life of Jesus. Jesus, he wrote, acted within the framework of the divine plan. Even Acts proclaims Jesus as the predestined Messiah (Acts 3:20), and the divinely ordained Judge of the living and the dead (10:42).[89]

(ii) The Divine Purpose: God's Plan for the History of the World

Pannenberg appeals to the notion of *the divine plan* in Rom 9–11 and in Eph 1:4–5. Among the post-biblical writers, he also appeals to Thomas Aquinas, who associates predestination and purpose with the incarnation of Jesus Christ. Predictably he also alluded to Karl Barth's grasp of the relation between Jesus and the *whole of God's history* with humanity. Even Schleiermacher, he said, emphasized divine predestination with remarkable clarity. He writes, "Jesus is for Luke the ruling centre of history by virtue of his divine predestination."[90] He further comments, "The universal significance of Jesus for the history of humanity is expressed by referring his appearance to God's plan for history."[91] Meanwhile, humanity in God's image is God's viceroy in the world.

At the beginning of this final section, Pannenberg writes, "The formulations of Ephesians and the Pauline or Lucan theologies of history have already given . . . answers to the question of the divine plan for history leading to Jesus

89. Pannenberg, *JGM*, 379–80.

90. Pannenberg, *JGM*, 379.

91. Pannenberg, *JGM*, 381; cf. also 386–89.

Christ . . . and the Lordship of Jesus over the cosmos, as is expressed in the formula of the creation of all things, not just 'toward him', but also 'through him'."[92] When he explains Christ's predestination to become the summation of the universe, Pannenberg naturally refers to the hymnal confessions of faith concerning Christ's mediation of creation in Col 1:15–20 and Heb 1:2–3. Christ is the firstborn of creation (Col 1:15) and the head of creation (Col 1:18).

Pannenberg writes, "The eschatological turning point of the world [is] accomplished in Jesus' exaltation."[93] Finally, he concludes, "The royal Lordship of Jesus Christ, the exercise of God's omnipotence in the world by the exalted Lord, . . . only in this light can we intimate what the incarnation of God in Jesus of Nazareth means: only in Jesus, indeed, only in the light of the eschatological event of his resurrection, is the eternal Son of God present in time. Only through Jesus is creation mediated into sonship, i.e., into its appropriate relation to God, and thus reconciled with God."[94]

QUESTIONS FOR DISCUSSION

1. In what does Pannenberg suggest the authority of Jesus Christ might lie?

2. Does it surprise us that Pannenberg prepares a Christology "from below"?

3. How convincing is what Pannenberg argues about the "facticity" of the resurrection of Jesus Christ? What does he make of the "empty tomb" tradition?

4. How helpful is it that Pannenberg insists that God is Father only through his relation to the Son, and that

92. Pannenberg, *JGM*, 391.
93. Pannenberg, *JGM*, 393.
94. Pannenberg, *JGM*, 396.

Jesus is Son only vis-à-vis the Father? How much of a breakthrough is it to insist that "person" is a *relational* term?

5. How convincing is Pannenberg's suggestions about the three offices of Christ as Prophet, Priest, and King?

6. Does Pannenberg put to rest traditional criticisms of the doctrine of the death of Christ as penal substitution?

7. How useful is Pannenberg's discussion of the so-called two-natures Christology? Is his contrast between the unity, disjunction, and interpenetration between the two natures helpful?

5

THE HUMAN CONDITION

LIFE IN THE WORLD, ALIENATION,
AND SIN

ALTHOUGH PANNENBERG IS WELL-KNOWN for his distinctive and major work *Jesus—God and Man* (415 pages), his later book *Anthropology in Theological Perspective* is more than a hundred pages longer (552 pages). In addition to this, much of the second volume of his *Systematic Theology* (more than 275 pages) is devoted to this subject, as well as his smaller book, *What Is Man?* The two larger works are quite brilliant, and outstanding in their scope and originality.

1. CREATION, THE IMAGE OF GOD, AND PRESERVATION

Christian tradition emphasizes the uniqueness of humankind. Secular thinkers often ignore this, in particular the *behaviorist tradition,* which stemmed from John B. Watson (1878–1958) in 1913.[1] Watson relied heavily on the stimulus-response approach. Philosopher Jürgen Habermas (1929–) emphasizes the uncertainty of the stimulus-response connection.[2] Humankind is not equivalent to the observable behavior that belongs to the purely physical nature of human beings. Pannenberg concurs and rightly refers to behaviorism as resting on discredited metaphysics. Animals are guided largely by instincts; the image of God guides human beings.[3] This implies that the image of God is not a static state of being something leading us towards a goal. J. G. Herder (1744–1803) believed that we are not yet men, but are daily *becoming* so.

(i) The Uniqueness of Humankind and the Image of God

The theology of the Reformation regarded the image of God as reflecting our actual relation to God. Pannenberg cites Martin Luther at this point.[4] More recently Karl Barth and Emil Brunner (1889–1966) debated whether the image of God was completely lost in the fall of humankind, or whether, as Brunner claimed, a remnant of this image was left. Brunner argued that such realities as the possibility of repentance and the ordinances of the state and marriage

1. Watson, *Behaviorism,* especially chapter 2.

2. Pannenberg, *Anthropology,* 31.

3. Pannenberg, *Anthropology,* 45; and Pannenberg, *What Is Man?* 4.

4. Pannenberg, *Anthropology,* 49.

suggested that a remnant of God's image remained even after the fall of humanity.

Pannenberg rejects the fashion in much modern theology of speaking of an "'evolving image of God', which in many respects anticipates the evolutionary perspective of modern biology."[5] He agrees with the Reformers in identifying "our image" with "our likeness" in Gen 1:26, 28. These terms probably reflect Hebraic synonymous parallelism. Pannenberg comments, "The decisive question is . . . whether the image of God is to be regarded as having been realised in the beginning, and then lost through sin."[6]

On the other hand, Karl Barth objected to all views that link this image with any quality and endowment of human beings themselves. This implies a measure of dissent from Herder, whom Pannenberg discusses. Pannenberg argues, "The capacity of human beings for objectivity, for dwelling on the other as other, contains an element of self-transcendence, and elements of disregard for their own impulses."[7] He identifies human *self-transcendence* with the concept of *openness to the world*, which most contemporary theological anthropologists regard as a key characteristic of humankind.

This has special importance for Pannenberg. This is so because it implies "that in a specific way human beings [exist] exocentrically or *extra se* ['outside themselves']."[8] Such a capacity, he insists, does not apply solely to the religious side of their practical life. All the same, this is precisely a description of the essential structure of faith as trust. Luther argued that whenever we trust, we abandon ourselves, and build on the person or thing in which we trust.

5. Pannenberg, *Anthropology*, 50.

6. Pannenberg, *Anthropology*, 59.

7. Pannenberg, *Anthropology*, 62.

8. Pannenberg, *Anthropology*, 71.

(ii) Revelation to the World as Expressing the Image of God

The accusation is often made that in the Jewish-Christian tradition humanity is destined *to rule over* the earth, and that has promoted a destructive development that constitutes a threat to the environment, leading to reckless technological exploitation of the environment. This is precisely the concern that Jürgen Moltmann expressed in his book *God in Creation,* in which he spoke of "the crisis of domination" in "the ecological crisis."[9] In place of "rule," he used the term "*stewardship*." This was argued earlier by Reinhold Niebuhr, when he also dissociated "rule" from "mastery." He wrote, "Man's pride and will-to-power disturb the harmony of creation . . . in an effort to usurp the place of God."[10]

Pannenberg does not follow the pattern used by many theologians over the centuries of specifying a number of distinct qualities or aspects that combine to make up the image of God.[11] He rightly regards the image of God *as a whole*, and as a vocation or calling for humankind to perform. This is a demand to represent the character of God to the world. If we recall the pattern adopted by many non-Christian religions, often an image of their deity would be displayed in temples to represent particular qualities of the deity whom they worshipped. In like manner, God called humanity, especially Israel and the Christian church, to reveal to the world the character of God, whether this involves kingship (from which the concept of "rule" is derived), or such qualities as rationality, freedom, and relationality, i.e., the capacity to form and enjoy relationships with others.

In this respect Pannenberg follows Moltmann, who wrote, "The creation of God's image on earth means that

---

9. Moltmann, *God in Creation*, 20, 23, and throughout.

10. Niebuhr, *The Nature and Destiny of Man*, vol. 1, 191.

11. E.g., Migliore, *Faith Seeking Understanding*, 120–30.

in his work God finds, as it were, the mirror in which he recognises his own countenance—a correspondence which resembles him."[12] Additionally, the Orthodox theologian Vladimir Lossky (1903–58) stresses that the image of God is something into which we grow by divine grace. To bear the image of God, he argues, constitutes the difference between "an individual" and "a person." He writes, "*Individual* and *person* mean opposite things. . . . Person . . . distinguishes it [the self] from nature. . . . Person is a relational term."[13] Persons, he says, enter into relationships with others, and the image of God needs to be restored *by grace*, rather than simply being a possession by nature or birth. Such a view coheres well with the argument of D. J. A. Clines that the Hebrew of Gen 1:26 should more accurately be translated, "created *as* his image" (Hebrew *be*, with Hebrew "*beth* of essence").[14]

Pannenberg would agree with Lossky (and Paul) that the image of God is brought to focus in the person of Jesus Christ (2 Cor 4:4; Col 1:15).[15] Pannenberg writes, "The commission of dominion that is given to human beings in the account of the creation in Genesis finds its full realisation only in the Sonship of Jesus, that is, in the way which Jesus the Son of the Father perceived his relation to the world, and in which the relation is continued in the Lordship of the risen Christ. . . . The image of the second Adam (1 Cor. 15:49)."[16]

---

12. Moltmann, *God in Creation*, 77

13. Lossky, *The Mystical Theology of the Eastern Church*, 121.

14. Clines, "The Image of God," 75.

15. Pannenberg, *Anthropology*, 75.

16. Pannenberg, *Anthropology*, 79.

(iii) Creation, Its Variety, and the Work of God the Son

In his *Systematic Theology*, Pannenberg is concerned to show that the origin of creation is the free act of God, and not at all the result of divine emanation. Moreover, creation represents not a deleterious action of the Father, Son, and Holy Spirit.[17] He writes, "Linking intra-trinitarian relations to the idea of God's action as Creator, Sustainer, Reconciler, and Consummator of a world of creatures makes possible a clarification of . . . difficulties."[18] Like Gerhard von Rad, he regards creation as the beginning of covenant history. Scriptures speak freely and expressly of a variety of divine acts. God's creative action provides the basis for his claim to worship (Exod 20:3 and Deut 6:14–15). He sustains world-order, as well as bringing something new in history. Pannenberg writes, "This unlimited freedom of the creative action later found expression in the formula 'creation out of nothing.'"[19] God's status as sole creator of the universe excludes the dualistic idea of an eternal antithesis to God.

Pannenberg explains, "Behind the biblical statements . . . there is always the fact that the creatures owe all they are to God's almighty creative action. Once having called them into existence the biblical God then respects their independence. . . . The patient and humble love with which God seeks his creatures is defined in the sense that they do not proceed from weakness."[20] Pannenberg stresses that the creator did not have to create the world out of some inner necessity, but all created beings "become an expression of divine love. . . . The very existence of the world is

17. Pannenberg, *ST*, vol. 2, 1.
18. Pannenberg, *ST*, vol. 2, 5.
19. Pannenberg, *ST*, vol. 2, 13.
20. Pannenberg, *ST*, vol. 2, 16.

an expression of the goodness of God."[21] Here again, this is reminiscent of Moltmann's words, "When we say that God created the world 'out of freedom', we must immediately add 'out of love'."[22] Indeed, Pannenberg refers here explicitly to Moltmann: the creation of the world is an expression of the love of God. The whole human creation becomes the object of the Father's love, he says, "because the eternal Son is manifested in them."[23]

A problem emerges, in the first place, because human beings do not accept their own finitude, but usually live in revolt against it. They seek unlimited expansion of their existence. They want to be like God. Jesus, however, accepted his finitude: "Jesus, then, put his own existence in the service of the glorifying of God."[24] This can be explained readily in terms of "otherness" (i.e., other than the self). We need to interpret the mediatorship of the Son in creation, and to resist the notion that this implies an anthropomorphic way of relating to the will of God and his creative action.

Pannenberg argues that Hegel's philosophy of religion offers a conceptual starting point for this understanding. He writes, "Hegel's thesis is that in the Trinity the Son is the principle of otherness, a starting point for the emergence of the finite as that which is absolutely other than deity." He continues, "Otherness, then, may be seen as the generative principle of the multiplicity of creaturely reality."[25] We need, he says, to think of the life of the Trinity in terms of the mutuality of the relations between the Trinitarian persons. This is why Hegel uses the term self-distinction, which allows for both difference and unity in the divine life.

21. Pannenberg, *ST*, vol. 2, 20–21.
22. Moltmann, *God in Creation*, 75.
23. Pannenberg, *ST*, vol. 2, 21.
24. Pannenberg, *ST*, vol. 2, 24.
25. Pannenberg, *ST*, vol. 2, 28.

All the same, Pannenberg insists, "God differs from both the Neoplatonic and the Hegelian views."[26] He is not simply repeating Hegel's ideas without qualification.

Turning to Scripture, Pannenberg insists, "The Spirit was at work in creation (Gen. 1:2), especially as the origin of life in the creatures (Gen. 2:7; Ps. 104:29–30). . . . The Spirit is the principle of the creative present of the transcendent God. . . . He is the medium of the participation of the creatures in the divine life."[27] He adds, "The work of the Spirit in creation thus converges on the Incarnation of the Son, which in the scriptural testimony is in a special way the work of the Spirit."[28] The life-giving Spirit brings preservation as well as creation, and a constantly new creative fashioning that goes beyond what was given with existence originally.

(iv) Preservation, Governance of the World, and the Goal of Creation

God wills to preserve the world. Pannenberg comments, "This divine provision for creatures finds especially intensive expression in what Jesus says about the birds of heaven and the lilies of the field (Matt. 6:25–26, 27–31; Luke 12:24–28), as God sees to the special needs of each."[29] God cares, he writes, for each individual creature, providing it with food and water at the right time (Deut 11:12–15; Jer 5:24; Ps 104:13–24).

Pannenberg declares that the divine work that follows "is of a different kind, i.e., the work of preserving and

26. Pannenberg, *ST*, vol. 2, 31.
27. Pannenberg, *ST*, vol. 2, 32.
28. Pannenberg, *ST*, vol. 2, 34.
29. Pannenberg, *ST*, vol. 2, 35.

governing what was created."[30] He continues, "the faithfulness of God guarantees as well as makes possible the emergence and persistence of continuously existing forms of creaturely reality and their ongoing identity."[31] While God is acting in preserving and ruling his creatures, he may also bring forth new things. God's faithfulness is shown only over extended time, which applies especially to the world. Pannenberg does not adopt the deist view that God cannot intervene in the course of the physical world and history. He accepts that there can be identity in change, and that self-preservation alone cannot guarantee the continuation of one's own existence and nature.

On the final goal of creation, Pannenberg regards *God himself* as its goal. He writes, "God sought his own glory by giving existence to creatures. . . . It, too, is an expression of God's love, and it has as its content and object the consolation of creation and creatures." He comments, "Certainly creatures can achieve the consolation of their creaturely existence only by praising and honouring God."[32]

2. THE WORLD OF CREATURES, CREATION, AND ESCHATOLOGY

(i) The Animal Kingdom

Pannenberg states, "Theology cannot refrain from describing the world of nature and human history as the creation of God, often claiming that only thus we bring into view the true nature of the world."[33] The world of creatures, he says, has its distinctiveness only vis-à-vis other finite things.

30. Pannenberg, *ST*, vol. 2, 37.
31. Pannenberg, *ST*, vol. 2, 40.
32. Pannenberg, *ST*, vol. 2, 57.
33. Pannenberg, *ST*, vol. 2, 59.

Creaturely reality is a plurality of creatures. This plurality is part of the concept of the finite. As the productive principle of diversity, the *Logos—the Son of God*—is the origin of each individual creature, and of the order of relations between the creatures.

Order and unity are not just external to the creatures. The variety within creation constitutes the generative principle of otherness. What are we to say about the laws of the universe? Pannenberg insists:

> The uniformity of events according to law is . . . a condition of creaturely independence. If the Creator wanted to bring forth independent creatures, he had primary need of the uniformity of elementary processes. . . . The uniformity of natural occurrence is on the one hand an expression of God's faithfulness and constancy in his activity as Creator and Sustainer, while on the other hand it is the indispensable basis for the development of ever new and more complex forms in the world of creatures.[34]

Pannenberg also asserts that the goal of creation involves the participation of creatures in the Trinitarian fellowship of the Son with the Father. The goal of creation is that all might be reconciled in Jesus Christ (Col 1:20; cf. Eph 1:10). Perhaps more speculatively, Pannenberg maintains that the relation of nonhuman creatures to their Creator thereby also comes to fulfillment.[35] Redemption and reconciliation may well include more than humankind alone. Many even speculate about the possibility of intelligent beings in other galaxies, whether or not they, too, need redemption.

---

34. Pannenberg, *ST,* vol. 2, 72.

35. Pannenberg, *ST,* vol. 2, 73.

(ii) The Spirit of God and Dynamic Creativity

Pannenberg begins with the biblical idea that the Holy Spirit is the *life-giving principle*. As we read in Ps 104:30, "When you send forth your Spirit, they [the animals] are created; and you renew the face of the ground." The new life of the resurrection is the work of the divine Spirit (Rom 8:11; 1 Cor 15:44–45).

In relation to the dynamics of creation, Pannenberg suggests that field theory in physics may be a helpful model or analogy. He comments, "The claim that the switch in modern physics to increasingly comprehensive field theories of natural occurrence is of theological relevance finds support in the metaphysical origin of the field concept."[36] "Field" theories, however, are not easy to explain to those without a scientific background and perhaps the best way in is through their development. Several decisive steps led to contemporary field theory.

First, Michael Faraday (1791–1867) developed Newton's theory of gravitational force, especially in his concept of the electromagnetic field in physics. Then James Maxwell (1831–79) applied Faraday's lines of force to electrodynamics. Heinrich Hertz (1857–94) worked further on vector fields. Paul Dirac (1902–84) of Cambridge further developed quantum physics and associated field theory. The cumulative result of this was to demonstrate the interaction of force-fields in space. From Pannenberg's perspective, this history offered (1) a more coherent model of Trinitarian action in terms of three interlinked fields of force or Trinitarian interaction, and also (2) the notion of God's omnipresence through his dynamic Spirit as reaching the furthest regions of the universe. The above is, alas, merely a

---

36. Pannenberg, *ST,* vol. 2, 81.

crude, rough, and simplified explanation by someone with little scientific background.

Against this background, perhaps it need not surprise us when Pannenberg writes, "Spatial ideas occur . . . in biblical statements about God's relation to creation. . . . The concept of the incarnation . . . implies a spatial difference that can be overcome only in the temporal process."[37] It is inappropriate, he says, to localise *God himself* in space. But we do not avoid this by limiting the idea of space to *God's relations with his creatures*. He devotes nearly a dozen pages to discussing historically influential concepts of space. The older "objective" view of space, which influenced positivists before the work of more recent physicists, is no longer a convincing paradigm.

More recent models emphasize the unity or relatedness of space and time. With reference to time, Pannenberg concludes, "With the completion of God's plan for history in his kingdom time itself will end (Rev. 10:6–7) in the sense that God will overcome the separation of the past, present, and the future. . . . [This is] a feature of cosmic time in distinction from eternity."[38] The Spirit is the creative origin of the new life of the resurrection (Rom 8:11). He adds, "A dynamic of the Divine Spirit . . . stands in a demonstrable relation to the basic data of science."[39]

(iii) Animals, Angels, and the Heavens

Pannenberg necessarily pays attention to animals and angels, because we do not live in an anthropocentric universe, and God is the creator of all reality. The New Testament speaks of "principalities and powers" (1 Pet 3:22; cf.

37. Pannenberg, *ST,* vol. 2, 85.

38. Pannenberg, *ST,* vol. 2, 95.

39. Pannenberg, *ST,* vol. 2, 101.

1 Cor 15:24; Eph 1:21; Rom 8:28). All these powers are set under the domain of the exalted Christ. He refers to Karl Barth's discussion of angels as the most important discussion of this theme in modern theology.[40] The early church fathers reflect the New Testament when they asserted the significance of the non-human creation. The Enlightenment tended to conceive of the universe and the nexus of nature as a closed system.

The first creation story (Gen 1:1—2:3), Pannenberg comments, depicts the creation of the world already as a sequence of forms. It is astonishing, he thinks, that there is much agreement with science in the biblical sequence, in spite of certain differences.[41] He comments, "More surprising than the difference in order at this point between science and the early Genesis story is the measure of material agreement between them. . . . Even more astonishing than these detailed agreements is agreement on the basic idea of a sequence in the development of creaturely forms."[42] Much of the Old Testament underlines the creative nature of God's acts in history. In biblical belief, he says, the variety of forms of life plays an important role.[43] The biblical writers found the variety and grandeur of these forms fascinating. The novelty of God's creative power finds expression in the Hebrew term *bārā'*, "created" (Gen 1:1, 21).

Sometimes humankind is permitted to have a share in the creative force that comes from God. One example cited by Pannenberg is that of agriculture. He allows for the "self-organization of living creatures," but concludes, "All creatures owe their existence to the creative activity of God."[44]

40. Barth, *Church Dogmatics* III.3, sect. 51 (ET, vol. 7, 369–418).

41. Pannenberg, *ST,* vol. 2, 116.

42. Pannenberg, *ST,* vol. 2, 118.

43. Pannenberg, *ST,* vol. 2, 129.

44. Pannenberg, *ST,* vol. 2, 135.

(iv) Creation and Eschatology

Paul points out in Rom 8:19–22 that the whole of creation "has been groaning in labor pains until now" in eager expectation for universal release from bondage, because of what Pannenberg calls "the contradiction between its state and the goal that he [God] set for it."[45] One day, God will set aside this contradiction. In Pannenberg's own words, "Oriented to the eschatological consummation, this creative presence of God in the imminence of the creaturely world and its forms has given us occasion today to speak of a 'sacramental' view of nature in Christianity."[46] Such a view of nature may be set consciously against merely *instrumental* or *secularist* views of nature. On the other hand, however, it does not allow us to step back into a veneration of nature. All creation is waiting for the manifestation of sonship in us.

Creation and eschatology belong together, Pannenberg says, because it is only in the eschatological consummation that the destiny of the creature, especially the human creature will come to fulfillment. The divine act of creation, as Augustine said, precedes time, and the precedents of the beginning and the end. For this reason, God is said to be the First and the Last (Rev 1:8; 21:6; 22:13). God stands above the alternatives of beginning and end, because he is Lord of both. Pannenberg attempts to link the thought that creation, as an eternal act, is simultaneous with the process of time, even if the act of creation is within time. Further, the notion that creation ended on the sixth day suggests that world history commenced then.[47] Pannenberg adds that an extension of the concept of creation to the whole history of the world

45. Pannenberg, *ST*, vol. 2, 137.
46. Pannenberg, *ST*, vol. 2, 137.
47. Pannenberg, *ST*, vol. 2, 141.

was pioneered in the first place in Jewish expositions of the seven days of the first creation story.

Pannenberg devotes nearly twenty pages to discussing the intelligibility of the beginning and end of the universe. He concludes that modern belief in the infinity of the world was partly a result of the link between the Copernican revolution in our view of the world and the geometric conception of space in modern science. It also owes something to the development of the mathematical theory attributable to Bernhard Bolzano (1781–1848), even if this theory does not relate directly to cosmology.

Nevertheless, Pannenberg argues, the difficulties relating to temporal beginning rest on the fact that the flux of time does not depend on material processes.[48] He takes account of standard models of an expanding universe, but argues that if we trace back the curve of the expansion to follow it backward in time, it leads only to a proximate point where mass is infinitely dense, and space is infinitely compressed. It does not lead to an explicit point at which time reaches zero: "Physics perhaps cannot determine the beginning."[49] He then examines related problems discerning the end of the world.

(v) Good Creation and the Problem of Evil and Suffering

Pannenberg is acutely aware that the problem of evil and suffering appears to challenge the teaching in Genesis that creation is said to be "very good" (Gen 1:31). So much suffering and evil appears to be senseless. Yet the faith of Israel and primitive Christianity never entertained the thought of accusing the Creator of any evil. It is quite the reverse: the creature has no right to make itself the judge of God's creative

48. Pannenberg, *ST,* vol. 2, 155.
49. Pannenberg, *ST,* vol. 2, 156.

action. Isaiah 45:9 declares, "Woe to you who strive with your Maker!—earthen vessels with the Potter. Does the clay say to the one who fashions it, 'What are you making?' . . . Woe to anyone who says to a father, 'What are you begetting?' or to a woman, 'With what are you in labor?'" Paul makes the same point in slightly different words in Rom 9:20–22. In this light, theodicy "cannot seriously arise."[50]

Yet Pannenberg is alive to the challenges that evil offers to faith. Suffering, guilt, and tears, he says, cry out for a real overcoming of evil. Nevertheless, he writes, "It is only God himself who can give a truly satisfying answer to this question. . . . So long as the world looks only at its uncompleted and unredeemed present on the one hand, and from the standpoint of its original emergence from the hands of the Creator on the other, the fact of wickedness and evil in the world remains an insoluble ritual and offence."[51] Pannenberg's stance is partially echoed in the work of Alvin Plantinga, who insists that merely because the *inscrutable* God has chosen not to reveal the reason for suffering and evil, *this does not mean that there is no reason*. Plantinga awaits the disclosure of God's hidden reason at the Last Day.[52]

Although he considers the responses of such historical theologians as Clement of Alexandria and Gregory of Nyssa, in the end Pannenberg's partial answer depends, first, on the sovereign and inscrutable will of God, second, on the futurity of God's kingdom, third, on the incompleteness and goal of creation, and, fourth, on the fact of human sin and alienation. This last factor is the subject of his next main chapter.

50. Pannenberg, *ST*, vol. 2, 163.
51. Pannenberg, *ST*, vol. 2, 164.
52. Plantinga, *God, Freedom, and Evil*.

3. HUMAN DIGNITY, UNITY OF BODY AND SOUL, AND DESTINY

The chapter in the *Systematic Theology* that Pannenberg entitles "The Dignity and Misery of Humanity" is without doubt one of his finest pieces of work. It becomes best of all when he examines what he calls "the misery of humanity," which we consider below, under 3. Both aspects, as usual, are supplemented by his work in *Anthropology in Theological Perspective* and in *What Is Man?*

(i) Humanity's Dignity, Destiny, and "Misery"

From the point of view of the biblical witness, Pannenberg points out, the destiny of humanity is fellowship with God, the author of the universe. He writes, "Only in the light of the incarnation of the eternal Son as a man, however, can we say that the relation of creatures to the Creator finds it supreme and final realization humanity."[53] This, he says, is the basis of the inalienable dignity of each human person.

The Christian tradition sought the basis of personal dignity in our creation in the image of God. Outside the Bible, admittedly, there are other ways of expressing the dignity of human persons, such as Cicero's (106–43 BCE) emphasis on human reason, and Immanuel Kant's basing of ethics on human nature. Because they have nothing else that commands respect, the faces of the suffering and humbled and deprived are enabled by the reflection of this dignity that none of us has by merit. Pannenberg comments,

> It is neither . . . oppression, nor the frailty and corruptibility of life, but human conduct, that contradicts our human destiny that causes the apostle to cry out: "Wretched man that I am!

53. Pannenberg, *ST*, vol. 2, 175.

Who will rescue me from this body of death?"
(Rom. 7:24).

> Mortality characterizes the misery to which
> all human life is subject. . . . The root of this
> misery lies in death's opposition to our human
> destiny of fellowship with God.[54]

Pannenberg considers various alternative terms to
"misery" but in the end he concludes,

> Misery, then, is the lot of those who are deprived
> of the fellowship with God that is the destiny of
> human life. . . . To speak of human misery is bet-
> ter than using the classical theological doctrine
> of sin to describe our situation of loss of this
> when we are far from God. The term "misery"
> sums up our detachment from God, our auton-
> omy, and all the resultant consequences.[55]

"Alienation," he says, has a similar breadth. We can alien-
ate ourselves from someone, and we can also be in a state
of alienation. Alienated from God, we live in the misery of
separation from God.

(ii) The Personal Unity of Body and Soul

Pannenberg is emphatic in resisting any dualistic understanding of the human self. Soul and body, he says, are
constitutive elements of the unity of human life that belong together, and cannot be reduced to one another. He
comments, "The early fathers defended our psychosomatic
unity as a basic principle of Christian anthropology."[56]

---

54. Pannenberg, *ST,* vol. 2, 178.
55. Pannenberg, *ST,* vol. 2, 178–79.
56. Pannenberg, *ST,* vol. 2, 182.

This reflects precisely the biblical teaching concerning the nature of humanity. It was only with Greek influence that Christianity inherited a dualism of body and soul. Originally such writers as Athenagoras (133–90) proclaimed that the Creator purposed eternal life for the whole person. Hence, says Pannenberg, resurrection of the body is necessary, for the soul alone is not the whole person. He rightly rejects Plato's argument in the *Republic* that the soul is divine. The Hebrew *nephesh* does not denote "soul" in Plato's sense of the word. Pannenberg remarks, "Human being as *nephesh* is a being of desires that are oriented to things that might meet the desires. . . . Hence ensouled body does not live by itself, but by the Spirit of God who breathes life into it."[57] The power of the Spirit gives to creaturely life an "eccentric" (not-centered-on-the-self) character.

In all three volumes on the nature and destiny of humanity, *Anthropology in Theological Perspective*, the second volume of his *Systematic Theology*, and even in *What Is Man?* Pannenberg is emphatic about the unity of body and soul in the human being. In *What Is Man?* He writes, "The distinction between body and soul as two completely different realms of reality can no longer be maintained."[58]

(iii) The Self among Others: Some Social Institutions

Only in the field of "*intersubjectivity*," Pannenberg remarks, does our awareness of a contrast between body and soul acquire some purpose or function. But here "soul" must cover more than the inner world of consciousness; it must include also the unconscious, which is related to one's own corporeality and its history.[59] In his *Anthropology in Theo-*

57. Pannenberg, *ST*, vol. 2, 185.
58. Pannenberg, *What Is Man?* 47.
59. Pannenberg, *ST*, vol. 2, 194.

113

logical Perspective, Pannenberg devotes the whole of Part Two (pp. 157–314) to the human person as a social being, and the whole of Part Three (pp. 315–532) to the shared world and social institutions. Initially he argues that self-consciousness can be developed *only in relation to the other,* or that with which identity is different from the self. Indeed, "Non-identity is indeed the starting point in the genesis of individual self-consciousness."[60]

Pannenberg discusses a number of philosophers in their approach to anthropology, and is often quite blunt, even if also accurate. He writes, for example, "[Thomas] Hobbes's [1588–1679] anthropological point of departure is . . . in theological terms the nature of fallen humanity."[61] On the other hand, many have advocated the priority of society over the individual in an exaggerated form. Jean-Jacques Rousseau (1712–78) bears some responsibility here, and neither Hegel nor Marx advanced appreciably further in this matter.[62]

We are on firmer ground with Martin Buber's (1878–1965) contrast between the I-Thou and the I-It relations. I-It relations tend to regard *the other* as *instrumental* or like an object; whereas in I-Thou relations the other is addressed personally as a *subject,* not as a mere object. Yet Buber has serious limitations, and remains prisoner of an over-sharp alternative. Even his later emphasis on language does not enable him to escape his self-formed prison. Franz Rosenzweig (1886–1929) moves forward, Pannenberg argues, beyond Buber's narrowly circumscribed world of personalism. He regrets the tendency of theology in the twentieth century to look more favorably towards Buber

60. Pannenberg, *Anthropology,* 157.

61. Pannenberg, *Anthropology,* 171.

62. Pannenberg, *Anthropology,* 180.

than Rosenzweig.[63] G. H. Mead (1863–1931) goes further in distinguishing between the self and "I," which is not fully absorbed by the social process.

Pannenberg also considers identity-formation. He considers, first, those who practice the psychoanalysis of Freud and his successors, and second, the depth-psychology of C. G. Jung (1875–1961). In his examination of Freud, he pays special attention to Freud's *The Ego and the Id* (1923). He discusses Freud's notion of childish narcissism, with its three components of trust, autonomy, and initiative, which supposedly correspond to Freud's oral, anal, and oedipal phases.[64] In particular, he recognizes in Freud the problem of how there can be a passage from the narcissistic pleasure-ego to what may be called the real ego. He has reservations about the process whereby ego and id are differentiated.[65]

In his subsequent discussion of the problem of identity, Pannenberg argues that individuals can modify roles and their social self. We may speak of the polarity between a *role* imposed by society and our own *individuality*. This is mediated through the perception of our own being as different from, or in harmony with, the identification imposed on us by society.[66]

Pannenberg's in-depth account of human identity and social formation includes a full account of the concept of alienation in such thinkers as Aristotle, Hegel, and Marx. We shall return to what he says about sin and alienation in his *Anthropology* when we examine these concepts in his *Systematic Theology*. Meanwhile he also examines structural identity and social relations in Part Three of his anthropology. He concludes that there are

63. Pannenberg, *Anthropology*, 182.
64. Pannenberg, *Anthropology*, 197.
65. Pannenberg, *Anthropology*, 200.
66. Pannenberg, *Anthropology*, 225.

difficulties and contradictions in our concept of "culture." But more positively, he also gives examples of successful institutional social relationships.

For example, marriage and the family "show in an exemplary way that individual institutions are not simply geared each to a particular need, but, rather, aid in the social integration of human behaviour."[67] Sexual activities, Pannenberg says, have the function of binding the partners to one another. The consciousness of time, and also feelings, he says, make possible the relation to their life as a totality. He comments, "The institution of marriage absorbs the tendency found in human sexual life to a lasting union with the partner, and imposes on it the form of a fixed way of life, which is entered into publicly and is sanctioned and protected by society."[68]

In earlier years family was often closely connected with property, but in more recent times this relationship has become less important. Relations between persons ought to be based on a free and reciprocal self-donation, and no longer subordinated to forms of economic dependency. Sometimes marriages become strained because there is unreal expectation that the experience of romantic love, which usually characterizes the early years of relationship, would continue into later years. At all events, Pannenberg observes,

> The validity of monogamy as the social norm in a cultural world that bears the mark of Christianity is nonetheless jeopardised today and has become extensively eroded. . . . The chief reason is the disintegration, in the public social consciousness, of the religious foundations of monogamy. In monogamy the communion entered

67. Pannenberg, *Anthropology*, 427

68. Pannenberg, *Anthropology*, 431.

into before God takes precedence over the
individual partners' expectations of happiness,
while the latter must depend for their fulfilment
on the mutual love that is grounded in the communion and arises out of it ever new.[69]

A further example of the need for social cohesion
arises because Christians are obliged to see embodied in
the laws of the state God's will that order be preserved. Pannenberg writes, "The seriousness of this will is manifested
in the present world in the authority that the state has to
punish evildoers. Early Christian theologians looked upon
the political order as primarily God's way of preserving
order in the face of the sins of human beings."[70] In this respect, Pannenberg follows the tradition of Martin Luther,
Reinhold Niebuhr, and many other theologians.

By now it will have become apparent that Pannenberg
offers a hugely varied and subtle dialogue with Christian
and secular philosophies and sociologists concerning the
structure of society and the formation of individual identity. It is unnecessary to follow all the sophisticated twists and
turns of the remaining pages in Part Three of *Anthropology*.
It has become clear, however, that this important volume
has no less importance than his distinctive and well-known
book, *Jesus—God and Man*.

4. HUMAN ALIENATION AND DIMENSIONS OF HUMAN SIN

(i) Sin Not Individual Acts, But Trans-Individual States or Attitude

In *What Is Man?* Pannenberg already speaks of the restless-
ness of humankind and his search for what is currently out

69. Pannenberg, *Anthropology*, 443.
70. Pannenberg, *Anthropology*, 448.

of reach. He writes that the origin of the whole of reality also remains ultimately unavailable to us.[71] He writes further, "Sin is something that belongs to man's givenness. . . . Left to ourselves, given up to our ego, we would have to smother in indolence or in arrogance, to consume ourselves in greed, envy, avarice, and hatred, sink into anxiety and despair."[72] Left to itself, he says, the ego would have to waste away: "The ego comes to be closed off toward God and thereby toward its own human destiny."[73]

Pannenberg writes that the human self retains its self-transcendence—or in his terms, its exocentricity—"but its presence to the other now becomes a means for it to assert itself in its difference from the other. Presence to the other becomes a means by which the ego can dominate the other and assert itself by way of this domination."[74] Everything else, he says, must be made a means to the self-assertion of the ego. All this analysis of the human situation is carried out at the level of anthropology.

In his *Systematic Theology*, however, Pannenberg discusses sin and original sin in an entirely theological way, and his discussion is, if possible, even more masterly. He rightly speaks of "the dissolution of the traditional doctrine of sin, especially the idea of original sin."[75] He speaks of "a preponderance of sensual strivings over against reason, as this might be seen in Romans 7:7–13, and 14–25."[76] In one of his most important statements Pannenberg asserts, "The decay of the doctrine of original sin led to the anchoring of the concept of sin in *acts* of sin, and finally the concept

71. Pannenberg, *What Is Man?* 33.

72. Pannenberg, *What Is Man?* 65.

73. Pannenberg, *What Is Man?* 68.

74. Pannenberg, *Anthropology,* 85.

75. Pannenberg, *ST,* vol. 2, 232.

76. Pannenberg, *ST,* vol. 2, 233.

was reduced to the *individual* act. We see this plainly in the failure of the theological attempts to retain the dimension of universal sin on the basis of the concept of individual responsibility limited to individual conduct."[77]

This statement goes to the heart of the matter. All the while that sin is understood as an *outward act* rather than an inward disposition of the heart, and all the while it is seen as a matter for the *individual*, rather than a communal or corporate issue, the biblical and Pauline understanding of sin will have little purchase and little penetrating power today. On top of this, as Pannenberg rightly notes, a purely psychological or social understanding of the causes of sin robs it of its genuine seriousness in relation to God. We must take account of the history of the decay of the Christian sense of sin if we are to understand what the marginalizing of the term "sin" in current speech implies.

All this is strange, as Pannenberg notes, when people today are well aware of the reality of evil. He explains, "The problem is that of our inability to master the fact of evil that manifests itself in its destructive effects. The turning away from God has made the problem all the more severe, for it means that we alone, and not the Creator, are now responsible for evil in the world."[78] We place the blame for sin on the social system or on other people.

(ii) The Biblical Vocabulary for Sin: Alienation and Death

Pannenberg rightly looks to the Old Testament vocabulary for the three main words for human sin, especially sin against God. The Hebrew term which most distinctively signifies revolt or rebellion against the underlying authority or norm is the Hebrew term *pesha'*, sometimes

77. Pannenberg, *ST*, vol. 2, 234 (my italics).
78. Pannenberg, *ST*, vol. 2, 236–37.

translated "apostasy." This is the case in Isa 1:2, where "All of God's people are in a state of apostasy and revolt against their God (cf. Jer. 2:29; Hos. 8:1; Amos 4:4)."[79] 1 Kings 12:12–33 also refers to Israel's rebellion against the house of David. Such a concept is miles away from "doing no harm to my neighbor" today. It relates sin essentially to God and our attitude to God.

The Hebrew term ḥāṭā regularly denotes sin of omission or an error, which in the modern world approximates to our notion of failure. It is the most general word for "to go wrong, sin, . . . commit a mistake or error, miss the way, . . . miss the path of duty."[80] The term may also denote offences (Gen 4:2, 22; 50:17).

The third main term is ʿāwôn, wickedness, denoting state or orientation. I have given an extended discussion to these three terms and their distinctive meaning in my *Systematic Theology* and my *Companion to Christian Theology*.[81] One term emphasizes the problem of straying from commands and disobedience; the second term emphasizes being alienated or in a state of being which is in a wrong relationship with God; and the third term emphasizes the resultant condition, which occurs about seventy-four times in the Old Testament, and includes the unsettling and destructive effects that bring harm, distortion, deception, and calamity.

Pannenberg declares, "The power of sin over us humans rests on the fact that it promises us life, a fuller and richer life. As we have said, this is its deception (Rom. 7:11)."[82] It de-

79. Pannenberg, *ST,* vol. 2, 239.

80. BDB, 306–10; and Klaus Koch, "*Chāṭā*" in *TDOT,* vol. 4, 309–19.

81. Thiselton, *Systematic Theology,* 148–51, and Thiselton, *The Thiselton Companion to Christian Theology,* 769–73.

82. Pannenberg, *ST,* vol. 2, 265.

ceives us, because although it promises life, it leads to death. In a crucially important statement, Pannenberg asserts, "The classical significance of Augustine for the Christian doctrine of sin consists in the fact that he viewed and analyzed the Pauline link between sin and desire more deeply than Christian theology had hitherto managed to do. The many aspects of his teaching that call for criticism should not blind us to this extraordinary achievement."[83]

Paul adds that the law becomes a means whereby sin achieves dominion, setting life before our eyes, but in such a way as to set the law aside. The inner logic of the link between sin and death as Paul stated it arises on the presupposition that all life comes from God; to be estranged from God means to be estranged from life. Pannenberg rejects the stark alternative proposed by Bultmann of understanding death either as a natural consequence of sin or as an imposed punishment.

Yet the redeemed will themselves stand before God in the totality of their existence and glorify him as the Creator of their lives. Pannenberg writes, "The fear of death also pushes us more deeply into sin . . . [but w]e achieve liberation from sin and death only where the image of the Son takes shape in human life through the operation of the Spirit of God."[84]

QUESTIONS FOR DISCUSSION

1. How does Paul expound God's work as preserver of creation and as the one who is responsible for its governance?

---

83. Pannenberg, *ST*, vol. 2, 241.
84. Pannenberg, *ST*, vol. 2, 273 and 275.

2. What light does Pannenberg shed on the biblical language about humankind being made in the image of God?

3. What consequences follow from Pannenberg's understanding of God as the *goal* of creation? How does this compare with the Enlightenment notion of an instrumental view of creation?

4. Is Pannenberg right in selecting the word "misery" for the human condition, in contrast to many of the traditional terms for alienation and sin?

5. In view of Pannenberg's emphatic rejection of dualism, and his insistence that body and soul are a unity, what does this suggest about the word "soul"?

6. How important is Pannenberg's insistence that sin is not merely an individual act, but a corporate state of being and attitude? Does the biblical vocabulary support this conclusion?

6

THE HOLY SPIRIT, THE CHURCH, AND HISTORY

1. THE OUTPOURING OF THE HOLY SPIRIT AND THE CHURCH

(i) Salvation through the Holy Spirit

GOD'S SPIRIT, PANNENBERG WRITES, is "not only active in human redemption as he teaches us to know the eternal Son of the Father . . . and moves our hearts to praise God by faith, love, and hope. The Spirit is at work already in creation as God's almighty breath, the origin of all movement and all life."[1] He is Creator of all life in the whole range of natural occurrences, as well as in the new creation of the resurrection of the dead. Paul says that the Holy Spirit "dwells" in the people of God, as a pledge of the promise

---

1. Pannenberg, *ST*, vol. 3, 1.

that the life that derives everywhere from the creative work of the Spirit will finally triumph over death.

In recent times the exegesis of the New Testament has brought a fresh awareness of the relation between the giving of the Holy Spirit and eschatology. We find this in Karl Barth and Otto Weber (1902–66), Pannenberg asserts, both of whom called for a "new pneumatological realism in contrast to the common inclination to speak docetically of the Holy Spirit by making him a stopgap that always comes in where questions that are posed remain open."[2] The Spirit is genuinely a person and a gift, whom Jesus sends, and who glorifies Jesus, by teaching us to recognize the revelation of the Father in Jesus' words and work. Jesus Christ himself, he adds, is seen as a *recipient* of the Spirit and his work.[3] As the Western creeds assert, the Holy Spirit comes to us through *both* the Father *and* the Son. The work of the Holy Spirit culminates in the future in the human spiritual body of 1 Cor 15:44–45.

The work of the Holy Spirit is always a creative activity, which brings forth life and movement.[4] The intratrinitarian life of the Holy Spirit is eternal. In eternity the Son is the recipient of the Spirit, who proceeds from the Father. Pannenberg writes, "But only to the degree that the Son is manifested in creaturely life does the work of the Spirit in creation take on the form of a gift. . . . It is said of Jesus Christ that the Spirit is given him 'without measure' i.e. without restriction (John 3:34)."[5] He endorses Augustine's suggestion that when we view the Spirit as gift we see the

2. Pannenberg, *ST,* vol. 3, 3.

3. Pannenberg, *ST,* vol. 3, 5 (Pannenberg's italics).

4. Pannenberg, *ST,* vol. 3, 7.

5. Pannenberg, *ST,* vol. 3, 9.

fellowship of the Father and Son finding its deepest biblical fulfillment in the *mutual love* in the intratrinitarian life.[6]

Because the Holy Spirit is God's eschatological gift, Pannenberg insists, we participate in the eternal life of God. We also participate in the consummation, when God will be "all in all" (1 Cor 15:28). He comments,

> The gift does not mean that the Spirit comes under the control of creatures but that he comes into them and thus makes possible our independent and spontaneous entry into God's action of reconciling the world. . . . As the Spirit who "indwells" believers (Rom. 8:9; 1 Cor. 3:16), . . . He is always surely more than simply gift, namely, the quintessence of the ecstatic movement of the divine life.[7]

God gives his Holy Spirit to all his covenant people, as the miracle of tongues in Acts 2:4 shows. To many present the sounds uttered are unintelligible (Acts 2:12–13). Pannenberg comments, "The event of the outpouring of the Spirit thus involves a comprehensive account of the church as the eschatological people of God."[8] These sayings in Acts, he says, are remarkably similar to the Pauline teaching in Rom 8:14–16 (adoption by the Spirit as children of God), and the Johannine concept of the Son's dwelling in believers. The Spirit and the Son mutually indwell one another as Trinitarian persons. He adds, "The spontaneity of stirrings of the Spirit in believers is inalienably bound up with the individuality and plurality of their manifestations."[9] Further, he rightly insists, "The criterion of authentic spirituality is

6. Pannenberg, *ST,* vol. 3, 11.

7. Pannenberg, *ST,* vol. 3, 12.

8. Pannenberg, *ST,* vol. 3, 13.

9. Pannenberg, *ST,* vol. 3, 17.

confession of Jesus as Lord (1 Cor. 12:3). . . . The church is thus the creation of both the Spirit and the Son."[10]

Pannenberg offers some brief comments on the charismatic emphasis that has recently swept through the church via Pentecostal and charismatic Christian communities. He admits that sometimes the Spirit may act spontaneously, but comments that the Spirit's testimony to Jesus Christ "acts as a brake on the unregulated enthusiasm that readily appeals to the dynamic of the Spirit, and breaks free from the church's tradition and institutional order, as though it alone counted as a sign of spiritual vitality."[11] I have discussed this issue in a way that is compatible with Pannenberg in *The Holy Spirit* and in *A Shorter Guide to the Holy Spirit*.[12]

(ii) The Church and the Kingdom of God

Pannenberg points out that the description of the church as one, holy, catholic, and apostolic, became a theme first in the Catechetical Lectures of Cyril of Jerusalem in 348 or 350.[13] From the days of Origen, the doctrine of the church had not usually become an independent theme within Christian systematic teaching. The Reformers were the first to introduce the doctrine of the church into dogmatic theology fully. Calvin's *Institutes* of 1536 had no separate doctrine of the church, but in his 1539 revision he expanded considerably his exposition of the concept, and in 1559 gave it increased importance. The history of the doctrine, Pannenberg

10. Pannenberg, *ST*, vol. 3, 18.

11. Pannenberg, *ST*, vol. 3, 20.

12. Thiselton, *The Holy Spirit*, especially 70–131 and 293–500; and Thiselton, *A Shorter Guide to the Holy Spirit*, 27–58 and 157–84.

13. Cyril of Jerusalem, *Catechetical Lectures* 18.22–27; *NPNF*, series 2, vol. 7, 139–41.

believes, shows that the concept of the kingdom of God had more prominence and importance.[14]

Pentecost, Pannenberg writes, was "the starting point of proclamation of the resurrection of the Crucified and of his installation to a position of eschatological power as Son of God and Kyrios."[15] The church proclaimed Jesus' resurrection and exaltation. But the kingdom and the church were not simply identical. He comments, "The church . . . is nothing apart from its function as an eschatological community and therefore as an anticipatory sign of God's coming rule and its salvation for all humanity."[16] But if the church is the sign, it points beyond itself. He continues, "The church's nature is to be that of a pilgrimage toward the future that is still ahead. . . . The church, then, is not identical with the kingdom of God. It is a sign of the kingdom's future of salvation."[17] As an orthodox Lutheran Protestant he comments, "The community in its 'institutional' form does not control the presence of God's saving future. This presence becomes an 'event' in it by the Holy Spirit."[18]

Pannenberg carefully discusses Vatican II's description of the church as a sacrament of salvation. Cyprian had spoken of the church as a sacrament, and as a sacrament it points to a greater reality. Protestants, however, have had reservations about the term, especially since in the New Testament Jesus Christ himself, not the church, is regarded as a sacrament of unity and the one sacrament in general.[19] Nevertheless as a sign and tool of the coming kingdom of God, the church has its end not in itself,

14. Pannenberg, *ST,* vol. 3, 25.
15. Pannenberg, *ST,* vol. 3, 27.
16. Pannenberg, *ST,* vol. 3, 32.
17. Pannenberg, *ST,* vol. 3, 36–37.
18. Pannenberg, *ST,* vol. 3, 37.
19. Pannenberg, *ST,* vol. 3, 43.

but in the future of a humanity that is reconciled to God. The World Council of Churches Assembly at Uppsala in 1968 spoke of the church as the sign of the future unity of humanity. In the end, the statement of Vatican II seems to say more about unity *in God*.

The church's relation to the kingdom of God is established by the task of achieving an order of justice and peace in social life. Pannenberg comments, "The kingdom will bring the definitive actualization of an order of justice and peace in the fellowship of humanity."[20] Meanwhile, the church cannot be identified with the state, for the political order is essentially a legal order.[21]

Pannenberg discusses not simply church and kingdom, but also gospel and law. In his discussion of the relationship between law and gospel, he quotes Gerhard Ebeling as emphasizing that the context of the contrast between faith and law is essentially *the covenant*: the main contrast is between the old covenant and the new (Gal 4:24—5:1; 2 Cor 3:6). The law is not timeless, even if it is related to the promise of life (Gal 3:12; Rom 10:5).[22] He includes an extensive discussion on the relationship between the law and the gospel.[23]

2. THE CHURCH AND THE INDIVIDUAL

(i) Common and Personal Confession

Pannenberg considers especially the inner structure of the church. At first sight we may describe the church as the congregation of believers. This has been basic and typical for the Reformation concept of the church. Luther appealed

20. Pannenberg, *ST*, vol. 3, 49.

21. Pannenberg, *ST*, vol. 3, 57.

22. Pannenberg, *ST*, vol. 3, 61 and 67.

23. Pannenberg, *ST*, vol. 3, 58–96.

to the phrase "communion of the saints" in the Apostles' Creed to support this notion. There is truth in this, but Pannenberg also comments, "We can easily misinterpret 'assembly of believers' as though the church were merely a gathering or society of individual Christians, and individual Christianity on its own underlay the fellowship of Christians in the church."[24]

The Augsburg Confession insists that pure teaching and proper administration of the sacraments are the only condition of the church's unity and therefore of fellowship. No common government is necessary; only agreement on teaching the gospel and administering the sacraments. In view of this, Pannenberg argues, "Not every gathering of Christians as such or on its own can be called the church. The church is there only when the proclamation of the pure teaching of the gospel and proper administration of the sacraments gather the members of this assembly."[25] The universal unity of the church across the ages finds manifestation in the worship of the local congregation that exists in virtue of its apostolic basis, having fellowship with past saints and martyrs.

However, what do we mean by the term "local congregation"?[26] In one sense "The Eucharist in particular . . . is constitutive for the church, between the fellowship of individual believers with the Lord Christ present in Word and sacrament. . . . We can more precisely elucidate the concept of the church as the body of Christ only in relation to discussion of the real presence of Christ at the celebration of the Eucharist."[27] In summary he asserts, "Where Jesus

24. Pannenberg, *ST,* vol. 3, 100.
25. Pannenberg, *ST,* vol. 3, 101.
26. Pannenberg, *ST,* vol. 3, 109.
27. Pannenberg, *ST,* vol. 3, 102.

Christ is, there is the whole ('catholic') church."[28] Thus, both individual faith and the communal or corporate reality of God's people have an important place.

In spite of, or because of, his orthodox Lutheran tradition, Pannenberg willingly accepts where Roman Catholic theology has moved and softened after Vatican II. He is appreciative of Joseph Ratzinger (1927–), and recent reformulations. For example, he notes that the priesthood of all believers is recognized as a constituent part of Roman Catholic teaching.[29] He remains, however, emphatic about the place of individual confession of Christ (Rom 10:9), even if personal confession is also "assent to the church's confession of Christ and acceptance of its trinitarian faith."[30] To endorse the Creed of Nicaea and Constantinople, he says, is not to ignore the historical relativity of these formulations.

The Holy Spirit maintains the immediacy of a personal relation with Christ, but the handing-down process of the church also presupposes the truth of what it hands down.[31] We must rid ourselves, he says, of any antagonism between the individual and society. The Holy Spirit nurtures both.

(ii) The Work of the Holy Spirit in Individual Christians

Faith constitutes a pre-eminent way in which the Spirit works in the individual believer. Indeed, "Faith is a form of the way we relate to truth."[32] In Hebrew, he notes, the term for *truth* (*ĕmet*) is linguistically related to the verb "to believe" (*heĕmîn*).[33] Truth is constant, and therefore

28. Pannenberg, *ST,* vol. 3, 103.

29. Pannenberg, *ST,* vol. 3, 127.

30. Pannenberg, *ST,* vol. 3, 117; cf. 113–22.

31. Pannenberg, *ST,* vol. 3, 122–23.

32. Pannenberg, *ST,* vol. 3, 136.

33. Pannenberg, *ST,* vol. 3, 136 (same page).

trustworthy. But faith is also *trust*. In turn, the possibility of assurance of faith is based on *the promises of God*.[34] Stanley Grenz makes this clear in his chapter on Pannenberg's ecclesiology.[35] Pannenberg asserts, "The promise is for those who grasp it [God's Word] in faith."[36] He comments, "The Reformers constantly set faith as trust in God's promise in opposition to an understanding of faith as mere knowledge of something that one may have at a distance and without personal involvement."[37] Saving faith, however, does not exclude historical knowledge, as if it were an antithesis of it. Philip Melanchthon, Pannenberg noted, regarded historical faith as essential. He devotes a section to the importance of historical knowledge, but concludes, "Faith as a personal act of trust is referred to God alone."[38] It depends on God's revelation; it is not self-generated.

Faith, in Pannenberg's thought, is closely allied with *hope*. He says, "To hope as such there simply belongs a sense of the incompleteness of life as it now is, related to the confidence that is oriented to its possible fulfillment."[39] He alludes to the promises of God to Abraham as paradigmatic for faith (Gen 15:6; Rom 4:3, 19–21). The Holy Spirit creates and sustains a longing for the future that God has prepared and promises. Christian hope rests on faith. The Christian life is marked by "not yet." The Spirit lifts us out of the vicious circle of sin and death, and Christ frees us from the imprisonment in self, and lifts us above the self.[40]

34. Pannenberg, *ST*, vol. 3, 170.
35. Grenz, *Reason for Hope*, 160–62.
36. Pannenberg, *ST*, vol. 3, 140.
37. Pannenberg, *ST*, vol. 3, 142.
38. Pannenberg, *ST*, vol. 3, 152.
39. Pannenberg, *ST*, vol. 3, 173.
40. Pannenberg, *ST*, vol. 3, 179.

Further, faith is closely allied with *love*. Love, says Pannenberg, "is a force that radiates out from God. It is not primarily a human act. But it lays hold of us in such a way as to make us active, too."[41] To show love to God and to our neighbor is a matter of abiding in God, and being open to the Holy Spirit (Rom 5:5, 8:16; John 17:21–24; Luke 15). Our readiness to forgive is also a sign of love (Matt 6:12).

By love, believers are taken up into the act of God's own love for the world. Hence, love is described by Paul as the greatest among the gifts of the Spirit (1 Cor 13:13). Pannenberg's one warning is that if we equate love of God and love of our neighbor, this can easily lead to a moralistic interpretation of Christianity. In its most profound sense, "Love reflects the mutuality of fellowship between Father, Son, and Spirit. By love of neighbor we take part in the movement of the Trinitarian God toward the creation, reconciliation, and consolation of the world."[42] Love springs from the grace of God.

The biblical teaching about adoption as God children and justification through faith underlines the divine Sonship of Jesus in which love is the essence of the relationship.[43] The Reformers were right to argue that justification is a verdict, in which God declares us righteous.[44] But this brings about the closest possible relationship with God, in which the believer receives God's love, and loves God in gratitude for his grace. Justification is God "pronouncing [us] righteous."[45]

41. Pannenberg, *ST,* vol. 3, 183.
42. Pannenberg, *ST,* vol. 3, 193.
43. Pannenberg, *ST,* vol. 3, 211.
44. Pannenberg, *ST,* vol. 3, 223.
45. Pannenberg, *ST,* vol. 3, 231.

3. BAPTISM, THE LORD'S SUPPER, AND ORDINATION

Pannenberg's account of baptism and the Lord's Supper comes appropriately immediately after his discussion of the dialectic between the individual and the community of the church in his section on the Holy Spirit and the church. Neither of these two sacraments or ordinances can be considered appropriately apart from their ecclesial context as well as that of the individual.

(i) Baptism

Although Pannenberg associates the regeneration of believers with the event of baptism, it is vital that he also writes "Baptism integrates the baptized into the church's fellowship."[46] The event of baptism, he says, extends far beyond the life of the individual to the common life of the church, and is fundamentally an action of the church as a whole. Both baptism and the Lord's Supper are *sign*ificant acts, i.e., "signs of the nearness of God."[47] This is part of the reason why baptism is viewed as a seal (2 Cor 1:22), or distinguishing mark of the believer.

Pannenberg rightly expounds the theology of baptism in such biblical passages as Rom 6:3–11. It stands for the theme of appropriation of the death and resurrection of Jesus Christ. As Paul insists in the light of the pre-Pauline witness of the church it is essentially baptism into Christ's death. It links the fellowship of Christians with the death and resurrection of Jesus Christ, and sharing the destiny of Jesus in his dying and rising again.[48]

46. Pannenberg, *ST*, vol. 3, 237.
47. Pannenberg, *ST*, vol. 3, 238.
48. Pannenberg, *ST*, vol. 3, 241 and 249.

Pannenberg asserts that in the earliest church conversion took place once and for all in baptism. Nevertheless, he adds that one of the most important merits of Luther's theology was to reunite the inward sense of penitence with baptism, and to describe it as "the task of daily appropriating the conversion and regeneration once and for all accomplished in baptism."[49] He stresses that it is an act of God, made once for all. Baptism is there for all our lives. Baptism and faith belong together. The rise of infant baptism in the third century with Cyprian and Origen bore witness to what was already an ancient apostolic custom.

Pannenberg notes that the notion of baptism as somehow cancelling a condition of original sin arose in the Western church after Augustine. Indeed, the Council of Carthage in 418 decided that infants needed baptism for the remission of sins and without it were excluded from the kingdom of heaven. It might have been helpful at this point if Pannenberg had entered into dialogue with the Roman Catholic biblical scholar Rudolf Schnackenburg (1914–2002), who showed what a minimal part the theme of "washing" had played originally in baptism.

Although Schnackenburg was a Catholic, his classic book *Baptism in the Thought of St Paul* was translated into English and warmly commended by a Baptist, George Beasley-Murray (1916–2000). He devotes only seven pages to baptism as cleansing for washing, citing only 1 Cor 6:11 and Eph 5:26, excluding Titus 3:5.[50] His two major discussions concern baptism as assignment to Christ and incorporation into Christ (1 Cor 1:13; Gal 3:27; Rom 6:3), and baptism as salvation-event (Rom 6:1–11).[51] He writes, "All the baptised have been incorporated through the one Spirit into a single

49. Pannenberg, *ST*, vol. 3, 248.

50. Schnackenburg, *Baptism*, 3–10.

51. Schnackenburg, *Baptism*, 18–61.

body, the Body of Christ,"[52] and he makes much of the imagery of "planted with," "buried with," and "likeness to" Christ.[53] In effect, Schnackenburg's positive points closely accord with those of Pannenberg, and his New Testament exegesis is faultless and accurate.

Pannenberg carries out a careful discussion of infant baptism and believers baptism, pointing out that Reformed churches and Lutheran churches retained infant baptism because they regarded baptism as acceptance of God's covenant of grace. This covenant of grace was not for adults alone.

Pannenberg comments, "Baptism does something that even those already converted before baptism cannot do for themselves but have to receive, namely the definitive linking of the baptized to the destiny of Jesus. . . . Baptism can no longer be viewed primarily as a human act, that of the baptized, for none of us can baptise ourselves."[54] He does not favor what many today call "indiscriminate baptism." He says, "It does not follow from all this that all infants without distinction should be baptized."[55] He is not unduly troubled by lack of evidence for infant baptism within the New Testament, especially since that era concerns first-generation Christians. He emphasizes, rather, "Baptism needs appropriation by faith."[56]

(ii) The Lord's Supper and Christian Worship

As we might expect, Pannenberg begins his consideration of the Lord's Supper with the rehearsal of the pre-Pauline tradition of the institution of the Lord's Supper in 1 Cor

52. Schnackenburg, *Baptism*, 28.

53. Schnackenburg, *Baptism*, 47–55.

54. Pannenberg, *ST*, vol. 3, 260.

55. Pannenberg, *ST*, vol. 3, 264.

56. Pannenberg, *ST*, vol. 3, 272.

11:24–25. This institution, he says, is basic to the celebration, even more directly than in the case of baptism. He also cites an allusion to the breaking of bread in Acts 2:42, 46, in Luke 24:30–31, and in Acts 10:41. John 21:13 tells us that the risen Lord appeared to the disciples, and shared a common meal with them. Pannenberg also mentions the accounts in Mark 14:22–24 and in Matt 26:26–28, although he acknowledges that there is no express command to continue celebrations after the death of Jesus. But the Jesus tradition as a whole confirms an adequate basis on which the celebration of the Lord's Supper continues as his institution.[57]

Table fellowship, Pannenberg points out, was a real symbol of fellowship with God himself and of participation in the future of his kingdom. Jesus used the figure of a banquet to depict the eschatological future of fellowship in God's kingdom. He also rightly asserts that the Lord's Supper is a sign of the covenant in a covenant meal.[58]

In the context of the traditional four interpretations of our detailed understanding of the Lord's Supper, namely by Thomas Aquinas, Martin Luther, John Calvin (1509–64), and Huldrych Zwingli (1484–1531), Pannenberg, as again we might expect, adopts a Lutheran approach. Like Luther, he rejects a technical reliance on the Aristotelian categories of accident and substance to expound any doctrine of the Eucharist, although he acknowledges that Cyril of Jerusalem, Gregory of Nyssa, and Ambrose of Milan (337–97) did speak of a "changing" of the bread and wine by the presence of Christ.[59] Luther did believe in the "real presence" of Christ in the Eucharistic elements. He opposed, says Pannenberg, not the idea of change in the elements,

57. Pannenberg, *ST,* vol. 3, 283–84.

58. Pannenberg, *ST,* vol. 3, 287.

59. Pannenberg, *ST,* vol. 3, 296.

but the *particular theoretical description* of the process of change—i.e., transubstantiation—that emerged in the later thirteenth century. Following Luther, Pannenberg writes, "Christ's bread-saying ['This is my body'] denotes the presence of the thing signified in the sign."[60]

Of the three or more Protestant interpretations, Zwingli insisted that everything about the sayings of the bread and wine was *purely symbolic*, and that the Lord's Supper was simply a memorial of his death in mental recollection. John Calvin, however, took up the position nearer to Luther, insisting that Christ was bodily present, in the sense that rays of the sun might warm the earth. While Zwingli stressed that the Holy Spirit mediated Christ presence in the Lord's Supper, Calvin insisted that the body of Christ in heaven mediated his presence. It is traditionally said of Luther, as already noted, that he taught the "real presence" of Jesus Christ in the elements. This is where Pannenberg stands.

At the Reformation, the 1549 edition of the Anglican Book of Common Prayer was probably close to Luther, but the 1552 edition of the Book of Common Prayer probably represented either Calvin's or Zwingli's view. The final 1662 edition virtually excluded Zwingli's view, but remained nearer to Calvin than to Luther. The Anglican Communion today represents a spectrum of views, ranging from Luther through Calvin to Zwingli.

Pannenberg points out that there has been an increasing consensus and interest in the theme of *anamnesis* in the Holy Communion, i.e., the "remembrance" of Christ's death (1 Cor 11:24; Luke 22:19). Paul also adds that the church should "proclaim" the Lord's death until he comes (11:26). Pannenberg reflects the increasing consensus when he comments, "In the apostle's words we are *not* to see the thought

60. Pannenberg, *ST,* vol. 3, 300.

merely of the *recollection of a past event*, which, being passed, is remote from those present. . . . For Paul Christ's atoning death has lasting actuality."[61] This remembrance is the work of the Holy Spirit, and not simply mental recall. Intense research on the meaning of *anamnesis* has also brought clarification to Roman Catholic theology.

Like Martin Luther, Pannenberg rejects the notion that *anamnesis* means an actual re-offering of Christ, as traditionally in the Catholic mass, but nor is it simply mental recollection, as in Zwingli's interpretation. In much Christian theology today, the word is thought to represent a dramatic re-enactment of the death of Christ, although by no means a literal one. It takes seriously the Hebrew notion of "remembrance" as a more-than-subjective recollection, but not literal repetition. It somehow involves bringing the sacrifice of Christ into the present, in a way reminiscent of the Black Spiritual, "Where you *there* when they crucified my Lord?" It does not take the believer into the past, but brings the past dramatically into the present.

However, many Protestants would not necessarily agree with Pannenberg that it is: "so to speak . . . Christ's real presence in the celebration of the Lord's Supper." Pannenberg speaks of "a descent of the risen Lord from heaven with his transfigured corporeality . . . mediated by the words of institution."[62] Most would agree with his comment, however, "Inner-Reformation differences in Eucharistic teaching can be overcome only by exegetical recognition that the issue in the interpretative words, particularly the bread-saying, is the presence of Christ's whole person."[63] Pannenberg devotes a dozen pages to

61. Pannenberg, *ST,* vol. 3, 306 (my italics).

62. Pannenberg, *ST,* vol. 3, 311.

63. Pannenberg, *ST,* vol. 3, 313.

considering the offering and the presence of Christ in the light of the work of the Holy Spirit.

In keeping with Luther's emphasis on God's Word, Pannenberg also remarks, "Proclamation of the death of Christ takes place already when the words of institution are spoken at the celebration, but is never limited to these."[64] Remembering Jesus and his death at the Lord's Supper, he continues, demands an exposition of the saving event that underlies the Supper. Many Protestants today, including Anglicans, would also insist that Communion without any specific proclamation of the gospel is less than ideal.

(iii) Ordination and the Ordained Ministry

Pannenberg describes the Christian ministry as a sign and instrument of the unity of the church. In this particular section of his *Systematic Theology* we should do well to recall his involvement in the ecumenical movement, as well as in the Lutheran Church and his awareness of Edmund Schlink's doxological concern. He begins with biblical passages concerning the ministry, especially Paul's list in 1 Corinthians 12. With Luther, he believed that the special calling is needed for a genuinely public ministry. This involves "a delegation of the powers enjoyed by the whole community and by individuals to one person chosen from among them, called by a superior."[65] Pannenberg adds, "In the first beginnings of the church the authority of the apostles kept the churches in their faith in the crucified and risen Lord."[66]

On the other hand, Pannenberg argues, "The authority and form of church leadership in terms of the office of the bishop cannot be based directly on an order that the apostles

64. Pannenberg, *ST*, vol. 3, 332.
65. Pannenberg, *ST*, vol. 3, 376.
66. Pannenberg, *ST*, vol. 3, 377.

set up to appoint successors."[67] This effectively denies the Catholic notion of apostolic succession.[68] The "core of truth" which apostolic succession represents is the preservation among the churches of the commission given by the risen Lord for the maintenance of Christian life and faith.

The Lutheran Reformation describes the ministry predominantly as a preaching ministry.[69] Calvin detected the origin in the early church of bishops, presbyters, and deacons. Teachers and pastors were taken from the ranks of presbyters and bishops, and bishops simply presided over the College of Presbyters. Paul had counted the apostolic ministry among the charisms (or gifts) of the church. Pannenberg then insists, "The public nature of the church's ministry of preaching and leadership that relates to the unity of the whole church . . . means that ministers do not act in their own name, but on the authority of the commission to teach the gospel."[70] In modern ecumenical terms, Pannenberg alludes several times to the Lima report on ministry. Luther, he points out, did not regard ordination as a sacrament in 1520, although Melanchthon did this in 1530.

Pannenberg rejects teaching of the Roman Catholic Church that ordination confirms a permanent "character," i.e., an indelible gift of an abiding character, which lasts for the whole of life. Rather, with Luther, he regards the laying on of hands as precisely the granting of the gift of the Spirit for ministry.[71] However, in spite of differences within different traditions, Pannenberg's ecumenical commitments lead him to believe that these differences are "not insuperable."

67. Pannenberg, *ST,* vol. 3, 379.

68. Cf. also Pannenberg, *ST,* vol. 3, 392–404.

69. Pannenberg, *ST,* vol. 3, 384.

70. Pannenberg, *ST,* vol. 3, 389.

71. Pannenberg, *ST,* vol. 3, 397.

More notable is the "especially crass and blatant" contradiction between the nature of the church and the actual state of Christianity when the issue is the church's unity.[72]

The Lutheran Reformation, Pannenberg comments, never rules out in principle ministry to protect Christian unity on the universal level of Christianity as a whole. All doctrine is to be proclaimed with the claim to authoritative validity. This requires the Christian ministry, but a problem arises with the assertion of the Roman papacy concerning the primacy of the Bishop of Rome over the whole church, supposedly resting on divine right. Matthew 16:16–18 and John 21:15–17 have been used to support the papal claim to primacy, but both texts can be interpreted differently.

(iv) Election and History

Pannenberg rightly relates election and predestination in Christian theology to Romans 9–11 and to Rom 8:28–30. The context is Paul's speaking about God's plan of salvation in his acts in history. He comments, "Only a detaching of the statements in Rom. 8:29–30 and 9:13, 16, from the context of salvation history . . . makes it possible to link them to the 'abstract' notions of election that . . . have been determinative in the history of [the study of] divine predestination."[73] He dissociates himself from the more popular "abstract" notion of predestination in two ways. First, he points out that election and predestination are fundamentally corporate and communal in Paul, and not orientated to the individual. Second, he points out, as Karl Barth insisted, election is Christocentric, i.e., derivative from the election of Christ as God's Son and agent of salvation.

---

72. Pannenberg, *ST,* vol. 3, 411.
73. Pannenberg, *ST,* vol. 3, 444.

Pannenberg also dissociates himself from views of election that presuppose God's foreknowledge of the future trust and conduct of particular individuals, which would be a way of introducing human merit by divine foreknowledge. He argues that the act of election does not relate merely to the pre-temporal aspect of eternity "before the foundation of the world" (Eph 1:10). Rather, it relates to the eschatological future and consummation of the world.[74] He comments, "The election of the people was the chief issue in Israel's election traditions."[75] The eschatological destiny of humanity that is manifest in Jesus Christ is present already, he says, in the event of calling to participation in God's eternal election in Christ.

In Old Testament tradition, Pannenberg refers to the election of Abraham and Israel in Gen 12:2-3 and Deut 7:6-11. He welcomes the relatively recent custom of referring to Israel and the church as "the people of God."[76] The context of election is also covenantal, which becomes associated with the Lord's Supper in the New Testament. 1 Peter 2:10 also applies the concept of election and the people of God to the gentile church: "Once you were not a people, but now you are God's people; once you had not received mercy, but now you have received mercy." Pannenberg also comments, "What God does in election is not just an act of historical calling. . . . It also forms the starting point of the history of the elect, because election is reintegrated to a future goal."[77]

Election, in Pannenberg's view, also involves the notion of the people of God as God's "possession" (Exod 19:5), and constitutes God's self-declaration or definitive

74. Pannenberg, *ST,* vol. 3, 453.

75. Pannenberg, *ST,* vol. 3, 455.

76. Pannenberg, *ST,* vol. 3, 469.

77. Pannenberg, *ST,* vol. 3, 483.

revelation as the God of election, human destiny, and history. There is also the theme of right response to the righteous God, which is of universal human relevance and witness. He comments, "Universal mission is the reverse side of the particularity of election" (Isa 42:1).[78]

QUESTIONS FOR DISCUSSION

1. Does the apostolic basis of the church depend on anything other than a foundation of apostolic doctrine and faithfulness to it?

2. Is it correct to argue that the Holy Spirit works in the tension between the "now" and "not yet" of eschatology?

3. Does Pannenberg succeed in relating baptism and faith adequately? Does he rightly balance the individual and the community?

4. Does he achieve a right balance between the Roman Catholic, Lutheran, and Calvinist view of *anamnesis* at Holy Communion? In what sense do we "remember" the Lord's death?

5. Is Pannenberg's view of "the ministry" adequate, and what does he mean by the priesthood of all believers?

6. How useful are his warnings against a purely abstract understanding of election and predestination?

78. Pannenberg, *ST*, vol. 3, 493.

7

THE FUTURE, THE SPIRIT, AND ETERNITY

1. PROMISE, ANTICIPATION, AND INCOMPLETENESS

(i) The Promises of God, Anticipation, and Incompleteness

LIKE MOLTMANN, PANNENBERG BASES the reality of the future on *God's promise*. Pannenberg writes, "The concept of promise links our present, which needs salvation, to God's future, but at the same time it keeps them apart. For the promise is as such different from the consummation that is promised" (i.e., the fulfillment may come in a surprising or unexpected way).[1] The promises of God are Yes and Amen (2 Cor 1:20). Here lies one of the great differences between biblical eschatology and secularized forms of the hope of the consummation of society, such as Marxism and the

1. Pannenberg, *ST*, vol. 3, 545.

neo-Marxism of Ernst Bloch (1885–1977) in his *The Principle of Hope*, which greatly influenced Moltmann. Bloch is atheistic and Bloch's utopianism dispenses with God.

The second key concept in Pannenberg's eschatology is *anticipation* or *prolepsis*. Christiaan Mostert comments, "The concept of *anticipation* is essential; indeed, without it the future can have no relation to the present."[2] Like the majority of contemporary New Testament specialists, Pannenberg is aware of "the distinctive tension between Already and Not Yet that is typical of the situation of the Christian community."[3] The majority of New Testament scholars nowadays reject the so-called realized eschatology advocated by C. H. Dodd (1884–1973), even if they concede that the Fourth Gospel is perhaps an exception. In general they affirm the so-called "double-polarity" of New Testament eschatology, which affirms both "now" and "not yet."

In his chapter entitled "The Ontological Priority of the Future," Mostert points out that anticipation in Pannenberg is both epistemological and ontological.[4] Anticipation not only links but differentiates, he says, the present and the future. Pannenberg's work, he rightly claims, is unparalleled by any other theologian. It is the connection between the present and the future that makes intelligible the Christian claim that a particular event in history can be something of universal significance.[5] In terms of the theory of knowledge, or epistemology, truth proves itself for the first time through the future and is accessible by trust or faith.

Mostert writes again "Truth . . . can only be seen from the standpoint of its end. The higher stage will always synthesise into a unity the contradictions of the previous

2. Mostert, *God and the Future*, 89.
3. Pannenberg, *ST,* vol. 3, 545.
4. Mostert, *God and the Future*, 116.
5. Mostert, *God and the Future*, 114.

stage."[6] The highest stage or the end-point is that of the Absolute. This is sometimes understandably connected with Hegel. But the key point on which Hegel failed, in Pannenberg's view, was his unwillingness to see the Absolute in its futurity, rather than as a timeless present of his own thought. It is not surprising that Søren Kierkegaard (1813–55) also criticized this failure. Mostert comments, "Truth becomes a matter of anticipation, or openness to its future disclosure. Pannenberg sees this as the same as trust in God, whose reality awaits its verification from the same future. . . . Jesus Christ is the ultimate, unsurpassable revelation of God."[7]

The ontological dimension of anticipation becomes clear in Pannenberg's book *Metaphysics and the Idea of God*. In his chapter on anticipation, he writes, "Every assertion has an anticipatory structure. For its truth claim can be called into doubt and discussed, implying that whatever truth it claims is not yet definitive nor indubitably settled."[8] Even metaphysical assertions, he believes, are to be viewed in the sense of anticipatory hypotheses that are directed toward reality as a whole.

A paradigmatic case is the resurrection of Jesus Christ, which is made present to believers through the work of the Holy Spirit. On the one hand, Pannenberg writes, "The eschatological resurrection of the dead is viewed as already and actually having broken into history. The final reality is present: in the case of the resurrection of Jesus, this reality has a continuing effect through the presence of the Spirit of life."[9] On the other hand, the Easter message is exposed to overwhelming doubt. From the

6. Mostert, *God and the Future*, 118.

7. Mostert, *God and the Future*, 118–19.

8. Pannenberg, *Metaphysics and the Idea of God*, 94.

9. Pannenberg, *Metaphysics and the Idea of God*, 95.

perspective of the future general resurrection, the resurrection of Jesus will appear not only as real but also as the anticipatory realization of this final completion. Pannenberg writes, "Judged from the perspective of eschatology, this anticipation takes on the character of an incarnation of God himself in the person of Jesus."[10]

Pannenberg discusses the epistemological dimension in relation to Kant and Hegel, and the ontological dimension in terms of the relationship between being and time. In the latter respect he considers that Heidegger's work remains inferior to the analysis of the historicity of existence in Wilhelm Dilthey.[11] The superiority of Dilthey over Hegel appears in Pannenberg's essay "Eschatology and the Experience of Meaning" in his *Basic Questions in Theology*, volume 3. Pannenberg writes, "What formally seems insignificant may perhaps appear later as of fundamental importance; and the reverse may be true. The final significance of the events of our life, Dilthey once said, can be measured only at the end of our lives, in the hour of our death."[12] As a further partial analogy, Pannenberg points out that we grasp the totality of a song only as we think ahead to its ending.[13]

(ii) The Holy Spirit and the Yearning for Completeness

The work of the Holy Spirit constitutes a third element in the context of eschatology. Pannenberg writes, "Pneumatology and eschatology belong together because the eschatological consummation itself is ascribed to the Spirit, who as an end-time gift already governs the historical present of believers.

10. Pannenberg, *Metaphysics and the Idea of God*, 96.

11. Pannenberg, *Metaphysics and the Idea of God*, 109.

12. Pannenberg, "Eschatology and the Experience of Meaning," in *BQT*, vol. 3, 201.

13. Pannenberg, *ST*, vol. 3, 598.

Conversely, then, eschatology does not merely have to do with the future of consummation that is still ahead; it is also at work in our present by the Spirit."[14]

Among the "big names" in Continental theology, Pannenberg especially welcomes the connection between the Holy Spirit and eschatology in Karl Barth, a connection equally prominent in Moltmann.[15] Oscar Cullmann might be also considered. He writes, "The Holy Spirit is nothing else than the anticipation of the end in the present."[16] However, British and American authors have also emphasized this connection. Two of the more significant are J. E. Fison in his book, *The Blessing of the Holy Spirit*, and the little book by Neill Q. Hamilton, *The Holy Spirit and Eschatology in Paul*, as well as in writings of my own.

Neill Hamilton criticizes the work of C. H. Dodd on realized eschatology, of Albert Schweitzer (1875–1965) on "consistent eschatology," and Rudolph Bultmann on "reinterpreted eschatology." In his New Testament section, he examines what he calls "The Spirit and the Eschatological Tension of the Christian Life."[17] In relation to being God's children, believers, he says, wait eagerly for adoption, which is further defined as redemption of the body (Rom 8:23). He comments, "The not-yet-fulfilled work of the Spirit is the resurrection."[18] The Holy Spirit, he says, enables the believer to wait in a way appropriate to his future righteous state. He adds, "The eternal nature of God's love (1 Cor. 13:8, 13) as well as the eschatological nature of

14. Pannenberg, *ST,* vol. 3, 353.

15. Pannenberg, *ST,* vol. 3, 536; and Barth, *The Epistle to the Romans*; and Barth, *Church Dogmatics* IV.3.1, chapter 16, section 73 (ET. Vol. 11, 902–42); Moltmann, *The Spirit of Life,* 114–267.

16. Cullmann, *Christ and Time,* 72.

17. Hamilton, *The Holy Spirit and Eschatology,* 26–39.

18. Hamilton, *The Holy Spirit and Eschatology,* 33.

the Spirit's action in the present, provides the ground of hope."[19] A classic example is Rom 8:26, where the Spirit prompts a groaning after, or sighing for an eschatological fulfillment still outstanding.[20]

J. E. Fison observes, "It is the sense of present eternity 'in the Spirit' that causes the inevitable foreshortening of the temporal future by faith."[21] In a subsequent discussion he comments, "We are to 'become what we are'—that is the secret of the Pauline understanding of the way to salvation."[22] Through being-in-Christ God has already made us a new creation, but the Holy Spirit gradually shapes us into that which is God's future destiny for us. The Spirit comes to us as the firstfruits of the final harvest (Rom 8:23), and its first installment or guarantee (2 Cor 5:5). Further to Hamilton and Fison, I reached similar conclusions in my recent book *Doubt, Faith, and Certainty*.[23]

The term "firstfruits" is the agricultural equivalent of the commercial or financial term "deposit" or "guarantee." The gifts of the Spirit are "so that the church may be built up" (1 Cor 14:5). The basis of all this, argues Pannenberg, is the eschatological promise of the true God who is also the Creator.[24] He also writes, "This future, regardless of its hiddenness, is constitutive for human life as it now is. For we can understand our present precisely as a fragmentary reality only in the light of our knowledge of its ultimate wholeness."[25]

19. Hamilton, *The Holy Spirit and Eschatology*, 35.

20. Hamilton, *The Holy Spirit and Eschatology*, 36.

21. Fison, *The Blessing of the Holy Spirit*, 122.

22. Fison, *The Blessing of the Holy Spirit*, 153.

23. Thiselton, *Doubt, Faith and Certainty*, 127–42.

24. Pannenberg, "Constructive and Critical functions of Christian Eschatology."

25. Pannenberg, *ST*, vol. 3, 543.

Death may mark the transition between the present and the future. Pannenberg writes, "Existence finds completion in death either in self-exclusion from God, as in the sinner's case, or in openness to God, as in that of Christ, whose death is the free act of self-offering of his own life to God."[26] He speaks of "the motif of the incompleteness of the relation between acts and consequences in this earthly life."[27] Moltmann is especially helpful on the incompleteness of a death that is earlier than would normally be expected. Moltmann writes,

> Most people in the Third World today die in an unnatural, premature, violent, and by no means affirmed death. . . . Their life is broken off short, if it has really been lived at all. . . . Eternal life gives the broken and the impaired and those whose lives have been destroyed space and time and strength to live the life which they were intended for.[28]

2. APOCALYPTIC, TIME AND ETERNITY, AND THE DESTINY AND GOAL OF CREATION

(i) The Role of Apocalyptic

Paul Hanson sees three distinct levels of apocalyptic: first, as a particular literary genre; second, as a religious perspective viewing divine plans and purposes for the world; and third, the symbolic universe in which an apocalyptic movement codified its identity and interpretation of reality. It is seen in such books as Daniel, 1 Enoch, 4 Ezra, 2 Baruch, The Apocalypse of Abraham, 3 Baruch, 2 Enoch,

26. Pannenberg, *ST,* vol. 3, 557.
27. Pannenberg, *ST,* vol. 3, 567.
28. Moltmann, *The Coming of God,* 118; cf. 50–54 and 119–26.

and The Apocalypse of Zephaniah. Nevertheless, boundaries are fluid, and there are variations between different
examples of apocalyptic. Isaiah 56–66 carries the need for
divine intervention, and a new heaven and a new earth.
Mostert even suggests, "One can no longer speak of *the*
apocalyptic movement.[29]

The importance of apocalyptic emerged within the
work of the Pannenberg Circle in Heidelberg in 1961. Ulrich Wilckens (1928–), Rolf Rendtorff (1925–2014), Trutz
Rendtorff (1931–2016), and Dietrich Rössler (1927–) had
published essays in *Revelation as History*, in which they
regarded apocalyptic as the native soil of the proclamation
of Jesus, and as representing history in its entirety and the
unity of history.[30] In 1960 Ernst Käsemann had described
apocalyptic as "the mother of all Christian theology."[31] He
portrayed apocalyptic as the setting of the ministry of Jesus and the eschatological people of God, and an anchor
against eschatological "enthusiasm," with a realistic portrait
of struggle. Klaus Koch, Christiaan Beker , and Alexandra
Brown, are among the many who press the importance of
New Testament apocalyptic.[32]

Reflecting on the universal scope of apocalyptic as
presenting history as a whole, Pannenberg writes: "Speaking about God and speaking about the whole of reality are
not two entirely different matters, but mutually condition

29. Mostert, *God and the Future*, 35.

30. Pannenberg, Rendtorff, Rendtorff, and Wilckens (eds.),
Revelation as History. Although Pannenberg receives criticism from
G. Sauter, William Murdoch, and Hans Dieter Betz.

31. Käsemann, "On the Subject of Primitive Christian Apocalyptic" reprinted in Käsemann, *New Testament Questions of Today*, 137.

32. Koch, *The Rediscovery of Apocalyptic*; Becker, *Paul the Apostle*
and Becker, *Paul's Apocalyptic Gospel*; Moltmann, *The Coming of God*;
and Alexandra Brown, *The Cross in Human Transformation*.

each other."[33] Pannenberg further writes that God's self-disclosure will be final and complete, when the hidden meaning of the present will be disclosed, and God's vindication will be clear for all to see.

Much of Pannenberg's most distinctive emphasis on apocalyptic is connected with his exposition of the term "the kingdom of God" in the teaching of Jesus. Outside the Synoptic Gospels, the term occurs in the Old Testament only once (1 Chr 28:5; although perhaps also Daniel). Its clearest use probably occurs in the Wisdom of Solomon (10:10) and the Psalms of Solomon (17:3). The Apocalypse of Baruch also has a vision of a messianic kingdom (53–77). John the Baptist certainly stands in this apocalyptic tradition.

Pannenberg has regularly said that the kingdom of God in the message of Jesus is central to that message. In the coming of the kingdom of God, God will demonstrate conclusively God's kingly power and rule. He writes, "At the heart of the message of Jesus was the announcing of the nearness of the divine reign. . . . Jesus called this God whose reign was near . . . the (heavenly) Father."[34] He speaks of the broadening and transformation of the prophetic expectation for the future into the hope of God's Lordship in the coming judgment. In *Jesus:—God and Man,* he says, "Jesus would have been closer to being an apocalyptic than a prophet in the old sense. . . . Jesus certainly thought in apocalyptic categories."[35] He continues on the same page, "With full authority he [Jesus] granted to the men he met the salvation expected in the future."

Pannenberg also repeats the same themes in his book *Theology and the Kingdom of God.* The oldest layers of the New Testament traditions of Jesus, he says, speak of the

33. Pannenberg, *BQT,* vol. 1, 156.
34. Pannenberg, *ST,* vol. 1, 259.
35. Pannenberg, *JGM,* 217.

presence of the reign of God in the ministry of Jesus. But these stand alongside sayings that differentiate the reign of God as something future. In what sense the sayings can be reconciled is a major exegetical question. He suggests that we do not favor one side or the other, as if they were in opposition, but must "rather seek the uniqueness of the message of Jesus precisely in this juxtaposition of seemingly opposing sayings."[36]

Pannenberg does not find in the contrast here between present and future the notion of a future extension and completion of that which has broken in the present. He formulates the opposite view: in the ministry of Jesus "the *futurity of the Reign of God became a power determining the present* . . . since the coming Reign of God had to do with the *coming of God himself.*"[37] He speaks of the "all-encompassing" content of one's relation to God and the coming kingdom. This corresponds to the universality of history in apocalyptic. Mostert helpfully underlines these themes.[38]

Three further aspects of the apocalyptic legacy concern the importance of new creation, judgment, and resurrection. Mostert writes, "The resurrection of Jesus is of fundamental importance in Pannenberg's theology. Its foundational role in his Christology is clear from the structure of *Jesus—God and Man.*"[39] Admittedly language about its present nature and its futurity has to be stretched. *But this futurity is primary,* as we have seen.

In one sense God already reigns unconditionally through his presence, but such presence of the reign of God does not conflict with its futurity; it is derived from it, and is

36. Pannenberg, *Theology and the Kingdom of God*, 133.

37. Pannenberg, *Theology and the Kingdom of God*, also 133 (my italics).

38. Mostert, *God and the Future*, 38–43.

39. Mostert, *God and the Future*, 43.

itself only "the anticipatory glimmer of its coming." Further, everything depends on establishing Jesus' unity with God, and this can be done only through the resurrection. Pannenberg argues, "For Jesus' Jewish contemporaries, insofar as they shared the apocalyptic expectation, the occurrence of the resurrection did not first need to be interpreted, but for them it spoke meaningfully in itself. . . . *If Jesus had indeed been raised, it would have meant the beginning of the end of the world*."[40] Paul, Pannenberg notes, declares Jesus the first of many brothers, the firstfruits of those who have died (Rom 8:29; 1 Cor 15:20).

(ii) Time and Eternity

Eternity stands in contrast to decay and death. Traditionally in theology it has been defined in four ways. (1) Many have defined eternity in terms of *timelessness*. Parmenides, Plato, and many in Hindu philosophy as well as some modern philosophers have adopted this approach, although Oscar Cullmann, Richard Swinburne (1934–), and many others insist that this would exclude notions of purposive action and sequence. These are attributes in the biblical concept of the living God. One of Pannenberg's clearest discussions of time and eternity occurs in his early essay *What Is Man?* Here he firmly rejects such a view. God's eternity, he comments, is understood in this sense in much Greek philosophy. It results in a God who is unable to act, for, "In order to act, God would have to pass from rest into movement, and thus would lose his eternity along with his constancy. For the same reason, the God of Greek philosophy really had no attributes. The eternity of the Greek God is that of empty, eternal being."[41]

40. Pannenberg, *JGM,* 67 (Pannenberg's italics).
41. Pannenberg, *What Is Man?* 75.

(2) Some have suggested that eternity represents the notion of *infinitely extended time*. But this notion is anthropomorphic, and is often described as everlastingness. Augustine rejected this notion by observing that God did not create the world *in* time but *with* time. Time, as we know it, is part of God's finite creation. Pannenberg also rejects this view. He writes, "The truth of time lies beyond the self-centeredness of our experience of time as past, present, and future. . . . Eternity, then, does not stand in contrast to time—something that is completely different."[42] Some have compared this view of eternity to an elastic band which is pulled out to an infinite extent. It is an extrapolation of humankind's limited, anthropocentric, experience.

(3) Many follow the classic formulation of Boethius that eternity denotes *the complete possession all at once* of our ultimate life. Pannenberg broadly follows this notion of time. He writes:

> The truth of time is the concurrence of all events in eternal present. . . . Eternity is the unity of all time, but as such it simultaneously is something that exceeds our experience of time. The perception of all events in an eternal present would be possible only from a point beyond the stream of time. Such a position is not attainable for any finite creature. Only God can be thought of as not being confined to the flow of time. . . . Eternity is God's time. . . . God is present to every time.[43]

(4) Very recently, others have urged that it is possible to conceive of *additional dimensions or concepts of time or eternity*, i.e., additional to those which we might imagine. This becomes possible in the light of recent advances both in the sciences and in literary theory. Literary theorists have

42. Pannenberg, *What Is Man?* 74.

43. Pannenberg, *What Is Man?* 74.

developed concepts of narrative time in contrast to theological time. One obvious example is that of flashbacks or flash-forwards devices, without which fictional narratives such as Charles Dickens' *Great Expectations*, and many detective stories from such writers as Agatha Christie, would become quite impossible. Likewise, in the world of science in relation to the speed of light, time would undergo subjective changes, especially for astronauts. Such changes in subjective experience of time may seem incomprehensible to some of us, just as a three-dimensional world would be hard to comprehend for creatures that inhabited a two-dimensional reality.

Although Pannenberg explicitly favors the third type of theory, his view is also fully compatible with this fourth explanation. After all, we noted that he called for a view of eternity that lay beyond the self-centeredness of our experience of time, and for a perception of events that would be possible only from a point beyond the stream of time, such as God himself would experience.

The third and fourth approaches to time and eternity are by no means alternatives, but rather, can be taken together. Pannenberg has other discussions of time, which show his awareness of the relevance of physics and mathematics. He discusses Plotinus, Aristotle, Plato, and Origen, for example, in relation to these theories.[44] He also regards the duration of time as "decisive for the independent existence of creatures," i.e., their freedom.[45]

As far as human time, or time-as-we-know-it, is concerned, John McLean has recently published a book on Pannenberg with the imaginative title *From the Future*. He writes, "Ordinarily the future is seen as an *extension* of the past and present. In theology the emphasis is on the

44. Pannenberg, *ST,* vol. 2, 92–98.
45. Pannenberg, *ST,* vol. 3, 997.

novelty of the future; it confronts and runs counter to the present world."[46] He continues that Pannenberg sees time and eternity in terms of the "creative activity of God, the power of the future."[47] In contrast to most other notions of the future, McLean continues, Pannenberg contrasts the future found in secular futurology with "an emphasis on the novelty of the future . . . and the idea of a future confronting and not just prolonging the present."[48] In summary, "God exercises power from the future. . . . God is powerful over the present as the future is powerful over the present. As we confront the future, we confront God. The power of the future is the power of God."[49]

(iii) The Destiny and Goal of Creation

Pannenberg writes, "God is not only the Creator of humans, as of all other creatures, but has also elected them for fellowship with himself . . . as a people."[50] The end of history, he says, is also the completion or fulfillment of history as acts of God and human destiny.[51] He writes, "The idea of an eschaton of history that is both end and completion of history goes back to Jewish apocalyptic."[52] In all creatures, he says, there is a desire for a totality of life that they do not yet fully possess. He concludes, "The future of consummation is the entry of eternity into time."[53]

---

46. McLean, *From the Future*, 93. (My italics.)

47. McLean, *From the Future*, 100.

48. McLean, *From the Future*, 145.

49. McLean, *From the Future*, 139.

50. Pannenberg, *ST*, vol. 3, 582.

51. Pannenberg, *ST*, vol. 3, 586.

52. Pannenberg, *ST*, vol. 3, 587.

53. Pannenberg, *ST*, vol. 3, 603.

In addition to his *Systematic Theology,* Pannenberg discusses this topic in his chapter "Selfhood and Man's Destiny" in his book *What Is Man?* The self that is closed in upon itself needs to transcend its egocentricity by becoming incorporated into a larger totality of life.[54] He contrasts "the poles of self-centeredness and openness to the world."[55] He observes, "Man's destiny aims at the harmony between the ego and reality. This harmony remains unattainable for us on our own. . . . God himself, who deals with us through all things, leads us beyond our ego along the road to our destiny."[56]

Pannenberg concludes that those who repeatedly places their ultimate trust in the infinite God will live in a way that was appropriate to their transcendent destiny.[57] Ultimately, in the *Systematic Theology,* human destiny is bound up with God's gracious act of reconciling the world to himself. Reconciliation brings "future fellowship with God by participation in his eternal life that is still future for believers."[58]

3. THE *PAROUSIA*, RESURRECTION, AND JUDGMENT

These three events constitute the main content of traditional Christian eschatology. Pannenberg retains them in his section "The Consummation of Creation in the Kingdom of God," which is his final chapter in volume 3 of his *Systematic Theology.*

---

54. Pannenberg, *What Is Man?* 56.

55. Pannenberg, *What Is Man?* 59.

56. Pannenberg, *What Is Man?* 62 and 66.

57. Pannenberg, *What Is Man?* also 66.

58. Pannenberg, *ST,* vol. 3, 638.

(i) The *Parousia*, or the Return of Christ

Pannenberg asks explicitly how the eschatological work of the Holy Spirit relates to the return of Jesus Christ. He comments, "*The coming again of Christ will be the completion of the work of the Spirit* that began in the incarnation and with the resurrection of Jesus."[59] But the new life imparted to Jesus Christ at the resurrection and return relates to that of a totality, a new humanity, for which he is the author of salvation (Heb 2:10; Acts 3:15). According to 2 Cor 3:18, we shall be changed into the image of the risen Lord. This includes both the community of believers and the individual. He writes, "The expectation of Christ's return is not orientated to the appearing of a single individual, but to the making manifest of the vital nexus originating in the crucified Jesus of Nazareth in the light of the glory of God."[60]

Pannenberg rightly says that the issue is not simply the suddenness of Christ's return, but above all the fact that no one knows its exact timing or date. He appears in his *Systematic Theology* to omit any lengthy consideration of many of the details of the expectation of the return of Christ. For example, in 1 Thess 4:16–17, Paul declares, "The Lord himself, with a cry of command, the archangel's call and with the sound of God's trumpet, will descend from heaven, and the dead in Christ will rise first. Then we who are alive, who are left, will be caught up in the clouds together with them to meet the Lord in the air; and so we will be with the Lord for ever." Pannenberg is clearly aware of the *symbolic* significance of such imagery as "the trumpet." (Trumpets were signals to awake a sleeping army, or to convey orders in battle.) It is also probable that the phrase "in the air" refers only to the last surviving generation that is

59. Pannenberg, *ST,* vol. 3, 627 (my italics).
60. Pannenberg, *ST,* vol. 3, 630.

alive before the return of Christ. Pannenberg is more eager to draw theological implications from the *parousia* than to fasten onto the details of its imagery.

What is clear is that Pannenberg regards the return of Christ, first and foremost, in terms of *the completion of history.* In a 2003 study that compares and contrasts the eschatology of Pannenberg and Moltmann, Michael Gilbertson sums up Pannenberg's view as "consummation as completion," describing Moltmann's work in terms of "consummation as radical transformation."[61]

The second conceptual context is its close connexion with *Christ's resurrection.* Christiaan Mostert discusses Pannenberg's assessment of the delay of the *parousia*, commenting, "The delay of the *parousia* does not jeopardise the Christian understanding of Jesus' resurrection because it is the proleptic occurrence the final eschatological event, namely, the resurrection of the dead."[62]

The New Testament also urges the *public* character of the return of Christ, which fully accords with the emphasis on future fulfillment in the Synoptic Gospels, and the universal recognition of Christ's coming. Pannenberg, as we might expect, stresses the relevance of apocalyptic, especially in its emphasis on God's sovereignty and the consummation and the completion of history. He also emphasizes that this is the climax and consummation of the kingdom of God. In his smaller book *Theology and the Kingdom of God*, Pannenberg explains that in the main sense the End brings the definitive meaning of "the appearance of God's future in Jesus of Nazareth," but in a secondary sense it is the end of mere "appearance" to human eyes, in contrast to reality.[63]

61. Gilbertson, *God and History in the Book of Revelation*, 186–88.

62. Mostert, *God and the Future*, 52.

63. Pannenberg, *Theology and the Kingdom of God*, 127–43.

(ii) The Resurrection

The resurrection also accords with the final hope in much apocalyptic literature. The resurrection of the dead is essentially the power of the divine life. Pannenberg discusses the ambivalence of the Old Testament concept of Sheol: "For in Sheol they [the Israelite dead] are separated from the power of life. Yet the powerful presence of God reaches even into Sheol, so that even there no one can hide from him (Psalm 139:8)."[64] Nevertheless, the concept of the dead as "shades" in "Hades" bears no direct traces of a *hope* for the hereafter. Pannenberg emphasizes the difference between general hopes of immortality and specific hopes for resurrection. It is the intervention in history of the *resurrection of Jesus Christ* that decisively heralds the general resurrection of the dead. This is what ushers in the apocalyptic and Christian hope of new creation.

In discussing the individual eschatology of death and resurrection, Pannenberg examines Karl Rahner's thesis that "existence finds completion in death either in self-exclusion from God, as in the sinner's case, or in openness to God, as in that of Christ, whose death is a free act of self-offering of his own life to God."[65] The act of dying is part of our human situation. Yet for Paul what follows death is not simply part of our human destiny, but more. The first man was created a "living soul" (Gen 2:7) as distinct from the life-creating Spirit (1 Cor 15:45). Pannenberg compares the links between death and finitude in Sartre and in Heidegger. He adds that we can truly understand the links between finitude, sin, and death only from the standpoint of the relation between finitude and time.[66] We discussed

64. Pannenberg, *ST*, vol. 3, 564.
65. Pannenberg, *ST*, vol. 3, 557.
66. Pannenberg, *ST*, vol. 3, 561.

time and eternity under the previous heading so we shall not repeat that here. Suffice to say, Pannenberg regards resurrection as entry into God's eternity.

Pannenberg also regards the universal raising of the dead as a prelude to the last judgment. Its basis is not only the life-giving power of God through the Holy Spirit, but also "the inviolability of the relationship of believers with Christ."[67] Plato's doctrine of the immortality of the soul acknowledges participation in the divine, but this is entirely different from trust in the Creator God, who acts in history. As Christianity developed, theology attempted to combine the immortality of the soul with the biblical concept of resurrection, and the Platonic doctrine underwent changes. But in its original form it was hard to reconcile with the biblical understanding of resurrection.

Pannenberg comments, "The identity of [the] future with present bodily life is basic if the hope of resurrection is to have any meaning. This hope does also involve a transformation of our present life that will, we hope, mean triumph over its wrongs and hurts and failures."[68] The identity of the resurrection body may be different, yet it is still an identity. After discussing various patristic and Roman Catholic views, Pannenberg concludes, "Precisely this link between individual and universal fulfillment of salvation is an essential element in the biblical hope for the future."[69] The hope of the resurrection is not simply concern for Jesus as an isolated individual, but what he is in relation to the people of God as their Messiah. He is the first of those people to be raised from the dead (1 Cor 15:20). Resurrection

67. Pannenberg, *ST*, vol. 3, 570.
68. Pannenberg, *ST*, vol. 3, 573–74.
69. Pannenberg, *ST*, vol. 3, 578.

did not happen to Jesus *for himself alone*, but in his capacity as mediator of God's reign and redeemer of our race.[70]

We saw above in chapter 4 that in chapter 3 of *Jesus— God and Man*, Pannenberg discusses the resurrection of Jesus as the ground of our belief in Jesus' unity with God and his unique claim to authority. Jesus, we saw, is the first-born among many brothers (Rom 8:29); Christ is raised as the firstfruits of those who are falling asleep (1 Cor 15:20); Jesus is the firstborn of the dead (Col 1:18). The same Holy Spirit who raised Jesus Christ from the dead also dwells in Christian believers, and brings them into the new creation (Rom 8:11). Pannenberg writes further:

> If Jesus, having been raised from the dead, is ascended to God, and if thereby the end of the world has begun, then God is ultimately revealed in Jesus. Only at the end of all events can God be revealed in his divinity, that is, as the one who works all things, who has power over everything. . . . Only because the end of the world is already present in Jesus's resurrection is God himself revealed in him.[71]

Finally, to recap once again, Pannenberg says, the concept of the resurrection is by no means self-evident in meaning. Hence, following Paul, he appeals to the experience of being awakened from sleep in everyday life. He writes, "The familiar experience of being awakened and rising from sleep serves as a parallel for the completely unknown destiny expected for the dead."[72] As we noted in connection with the return of Christ, the concepts of the *parousia* and the resurrection are closely bound up together. Hence, it is in his section on the resurrection

70. Pannenberg, *ST*, vol. 3, 579.

71. Pannenberg, *JGM*, 68–69.

72. Pannenberg, *JGM*, 74.

in *Jesus—God and Man* that he refers to 1 Thess 4:13-17, 1 Cor 11:30, and 1 Cor 15:6, 51.

All the main teaching of the New Testament about the resurrection of the dead is implicit in Pannenberg's treatment. Language about the resurrection of the dead is largely metaphorical, but he affirms "the facticity of Jesus' resurrection."[73] He affirms the tradition of the empty tomb.[74] He regards the resurrection of Jesus emphatically as a gracious act of the sovereign Creator God, and resurrection as a pure gift from God. The tradition of the resurrection of Jesus goes back to earliest times before Paul (1 Cor 15:3-4). Resurrection is "conceivable" through several analogies. The "spiritual body" constitutes a mode of bodily existence animated and enlivened by the Holy Spirit, in contrast to the weakness and decreasing capacities of the "flesh."[75] As the creative expression of ongoing life, and the Spirit of the living God, the resurrection body will be dynamic and ongoing, not the flawless perfection of a static existence. I have tried to call attention to this feature elsewhere.[76]

(iii) The Last Judgment

Pannenberg writes, "Confrontation with eternity means judgment only insofar as they [human beings] have made themselves autonomous in relation to God, separated themselves from him. . . . Not least of all as sinners, we are in conflict with ourselves, with the destiny that we have received for our own existence at creation."[77] God is Judge, be-

73. Pannenberg, *JGM,* 89.

74. Pannenberg, *ST,* vol. 2, 357 and 358.

75. Pannenberg, *The Apostles Creed,* 96-115 and 170-78.

76. Thiselton, *The First Epistle to the Corinthians,* 1257-1306; and Thiselton, *Life after Death,* 111-28.

77. Pannenberg, *ST,* vol. 3, 610.

cause in his eternity he is the guarantor of truth and justice. As the kingdom of God is already present by faith, so the future of God is also present already as regards purging by the fire of the divine judgment.[78] Pannenberg adds, "The message of Jesus is the norm by which God judges even in the case of those who never meet Jesus personally."[79]

The judgment that is put in Christ's hands, says Pannenberg, is no longer destruction, but a fire of purging and cleansing: "here is the solution to the apparent contradiction between the statement in 2 Cor. 5:10 that all must come before Christ judgment seat . . . and what 1 Cor. 15:50–57 says about transformation into the new life."[80] He asserts that the light of the divine glory is identical with the fire of judgment. This glorification is the work of the Holy Spirit. Judgement is closely associated with resurrection, when we shall be changed into the image of Christ.

The reconciliation of the world through the history of Jesus Christ provides the eschatological consummation of salvation. In one sense, Pannenberg argues, believers receive justification; in another sense this consummation brings about the justification of God "as a loving and omnipotent Creator." This eschatological consolation "will bring definitive proof of God's existence and final clarification of the character of his nature and works."[81] He writes further that the question of theodicy (or the problem of evil and suffering) can be no real threat to eschatological consolation, we shall see that God and his councils are above all creaturely understanding.[82]

78. Pannenberg, *ST,* vol. 3, 612.
79. Pannenberg, *ST,* vol. 3, 615.
80. Pannenberg, *ST,* vol. 3, 619.
81. Pannenberg, *ST,* vol. 3, 631.
82. Pannenberg, *ST,* vol. 3, 634.

Pannenberg writes further that this eschatological consummation has to do with the overcoming of all wickedness and evil. This is reflected in the dramatic depictions of the battles of Michael against the Dragon and the rider on the white horse against the ungodly (Rev 12:7–12; 19:1–10).[83] We may note that the cry goes up in Revelation: "Great and amazing are your deeds, Lord God the Almighty! Just and true are your ways, King of the nations" (Rev 15:4).

This theme continues throughout the book, as in Rev 16:5: "You are just, O Holy One, you are and were, for you have judged these things." Pannenberg declares "The reconciliation . . . rests on the fact that God has taken away our death by that of Jesus."[84] Judgement is *definitive*, and cannot be revised or changed. "Only the eschatological consummation in which God will wipe away all tears (Rev. 21:4) can remove all doubts concerning revelation of the love of God in creation and salvation in history."[85]

QUESTIONS FOR DISCUSSION

1. How important is "anticipation" and "incompleteness" in understanding Pannenberg's view of the nearness of the kingdom of God?

2. Is Mostert's title "the ontological priority of the future" a helpful description of Pannenberg's thought?

3. Does the Holy Spirit nurture a longing for completion in the way that Pannenberg implies? Does he reflect Paul's language about the firstfruits?

83. Pannenberg, *ST*, vol. 3, 637.
84. Pannenberg, *ST*, vol. 3, 641.
85. Pannenberg, *ST*, vol. 3, 645.

4. How should we evaluate Pannenberg's view of eternity in relation to the four possible ways in which this concept has been understood?

5. Is Pannenberg's insistence that God is the goal of creation helpful? In what sense does the future hold out the possibility of novelty?

6. How helpful is Pannenberg's definition of the "spiritual body" in 1 Cor 15:44? Does it also expose the problem of popular understandings of "spiritual" and "spirituality"?

8

HERMENEUTICS, KNOWLEDGE, AND TRUTH

1. HERMENEUTICS

Pannenberg's essay "Hermeneutics and Universal History" has been translated and reprinted twice in English.[1] He points out, "There arose in the 18th century the special hermeneutical problem of the modern era: the task of intelligibly spanning the historical distance between primitive Christianity and the present time."[2] Without hermeneutics, a gulf, he says, has opened up between the literal meaning of the biblical writings and the historical course of events to which they refer. But the historical quest is a quest related

1. Pannenberg, "Hermeneutics and Universal History" in Pannenberg et al., *History and Hermeneutic*, 124–52; and *BQT*, vol. 1, 96–136.

2. Pannenberg, "Hermeneutics and Universal History" in *History and Hermeneutics*, 125; cf. *BQT*, vol. 1, 97.

to universal history, and includes the specifically hermeneutical theme of the relationship of the text belonging to the past to the present age of the interpreter. It was to assist the engagement between these different vantage-points that I described my first major book as *The Two Horizons.*

In addition to his essay in *Basic Questions in Theology*, volume 1, Pannenberg devotes about sixty pages to hermeneutics in *Theology and the Philosophy of Science.*[3] In the latter book, he discusses first general hermeneutics with reference to Friedrich Schleiermacher, Wilhelm Dilthey, Hans-Georg Gadamer (1900–2002), and Emilio Betti (1890–1968).[4] He sees Betti as a corrective to Gadamer's loss of objectivity, and discusses the difference between value-related interpretation and a purely cognitively orientated interpretation.[5]

(i) The German Hermeneutical Tradition

In point of fact, the list of writers in the German hermeneutical tradition in *Theology and the Philosophy of Science* is not dissimilar to those whom Pannenberg discusses in his essay in *Basic Questions in Theology.* In both treatments Pannenberg attacks "the existentialist devaluation of the statement."[6] Probably the four figures to feature in the latter book are Karl-Otto Apel (1922–2017), Jürgen Habermas, E. Betti, and less prominently, Ludwig Wittgenstein. In this latter work, Pannenberg comments, "dialectic and hermeneutic share the fundamental feature of being concerned with the analysis of the interrelation of wholes and parts."[7]

3. Pannenberg, *Theology and the Philosophy of Science*, 156–224.

4. Pannenberg, *Theology and the Philosophy of Science*, 157–69.

5. Pannenberg, *Theology and the Philosophy of Science*, 166.

6. Pannenberg, *Theology and the Philosophy of Science*, 179.

7. Pannenberg, *Theology and the Philosophy of Science*, 189.

He also discusses the inter-relationship between intentionality and meaning in language.[8]

In his essay in *Basic Questions in Theology*, within four pages of the commencement, Pannenberg refers to the hermeneutical work of Hans-Georg Gadamer.[9] He also rightly discusses hermeneutical works by Matthias Flacius (1520–75), Friedrich Schleiermacher, Wilhelm Dilthey, Martin Heidegger, Rudolf Bultmann, and Ernst Fuchs (1930–2015), as well as Gadamer. In other words, he discusses the whole of the German hermeneutical tradition.

Matthias Flacius came under the influence of Desiderius Erasmus (1466–1536) and Renaissance humanism, and followed Luther and Melanchthon. In 1567 he wrote his main work on hermeneutics under the title *Clavis Scripturae Sacrae*. The "key" to understanding Scripture, he said, was Jesus Christ. Pannenberg acknowledged that under such biblical critics as J. S. Semler (1725–91) a degree of "objectivity" was sought. Nevertheless, Pannenberg also quotes Bultmann's judgment: "The result [of such an approach] was simply that philology lost its real subject matter, the interpretation of texts for the sake of understanding them."[10]

Friedrich D. E. Schleiermacher, with Hegel, remains one of the greatest philosophical theologians of the nineteenth century. He provided a great turning point in hermeneutics, defining hermeneutics not as "rules of interpretation" but as "the art of understanding."[11] He insisted that interpretation should take place between two

---

8. Pannenberg, *Theology and the Philosophy of Science*, 211.

9. Gadamer, *Truth and Method* is still the classic book on hermeneutics, together with works by Paul Ricoeur.

10. Bultmann, "The Problem of Hermeneutics," 237; quoted by Pannenberg, *BQT*, vol. 1, 101.

11. Schleiermacher, *Hermeneutics*, 35–79 and 113.

complementary poles: the "divinatory" (*divinatorisch*) and the comparative. The divinatory dimension helps to understand the wholeness of what we seek to understand; the comparative is more objectively orientated towards language and grammar. If, however, it is used alone it has the danger of incurring William Wordsworth's disapproval when he wrote "we murder to dissect." Likewise, Wordsworth wrote, "Our meddling intellect misshapes the beauteous form of things." Therefore, Schleiermacher sought to avoid a purely mechanistic model of interpretation, earlier popularized by the deists, and the rationalism of the eighteenth-century Enlightenment.

Schleiermacher also emphasized the need for what he called "preliminary understanding," often called "pre-understanding," after the German term *Vorverständnis*. This led to the conception which both Schleiermacher and Friedrich Ast (1778–1841) pioneered called "the hermeneutical circle." Schleiermacher explained, "The understanding of a given statement is always based on something prior, of two sorts—a preliminary knowledge of human beings, a preliminary knowledge of the subject matter."[12] The hermeneutical circle is understood in two ways: first the relationship between the parts and the whole of the text or work; second, our understanding of the whole depends on an initial understanding of a part. Bultmann illustrates this with the need to understand a text of music or of mathematics.[13] If there is no prior understanding at all, understanding scarcely begins.

Martin Heidegger insisted that the hermeneutical circle is a major key to understanding, and is certainly not a vicious circle. Grant Osborne argued that it is more

12. Schleiermacher, *Hermeneutics*, 59.
13. Bultmann, *Essays Philosophical and Theological*, 242–43.

constructively thought of as hermeneutical *spiral*.[14] In practice, Schleiermacher, Dilthey, Bultmann, and Gadamer all promote this idea, and Pannenberg also defends it. In addition to promoting the term "the hermeneutical circle," Schleiermacher advocated the importance of hermeneutics for Christian preaching, an emphasis that Karl Barth commended. Finally, we must emphasize that the divinatory and comparative methods are complementary. Schleiermacher writes that if we follow only the divinatory method, we become "nebulists"; if we follow only the comparative method, we risk "pedantry."[15]

In spite of his sharp reservations in other respects about Heidegger and Bultmann, Pannenberg in principle endorses several of these principles of hermeneutics. He writes, however, on the other hand, that Schleiermacher relied too heavily on the analogy of an oral conversation, and common participation in humanity. He was too "psychological," and in the end, inadequate.[16]

Wilhelm Dilthey was in effect Schleiermacher's successor. He extended hermeneutics beyond the interpretation of texts to the interpretation of human life and human institutions. His major interest was on lived experiences. He promoted hermeneutics as essential for the humanities and social sciences, or, in German, for the *Geisteswissenschaften*.

Dilthey had commented of such philosophers as Descartes, Locke, Hume, and Kant, "in the veins of the [abstracted] knowing subject no real blood flows."[17] In contrast to *Geist* (spirit), he promoted *Leben* (life) and lived experiences (*Erlebnis*). Hermeneutics or interpretation seeks of

---

14. Osborne, *The Hermeneutical Spiral*, 1–16 and 366–96.

15. Schleiermacher, *Hermeneutics*, 205.

16. Pannenberg, *BQT*, vol. 1, 104.

17. Dilthey, *Gesammelte Schriften*, vol. 5, 4.

the rediscovery of the "I" in the "you." The interpreter must "relive" (*nacherleben*) the other's experience by stepping out of his or her shoes and exercising sympathy, empathy, or transposition (*Hineinversetzen*).[18]

Nevertheless, Pannenberg believed that Dilthey had too much in common with Schleiermacher, and writes, "The psychological intention of Schleiermacher's hermeneutic was retained by Dilthey. Understanding appeared to him, too, as a 'psychological imitation.'"[19] It is extremely questionable, he argues, that anyone can "empathise" with any activity of men of earlier time, simply by having the same psychic nature, whether they be criminals, founders of religion, or rulers.[20] But he agrees with Dilthey that introspection is also an inadequate foundation of bridge for hermeneutics.

Bultmann, Pannenberg continues, fastened too much on Dilthey's appeal to human psychological possibilities, even though he tended to substitute an *existential* emphasis for a psychological one. Bultmann had based much in hermeneutics on "the interpreter's relationship in his life to the essential content which is directly or indirectly expressed in the text."[21]

Pannenberg further argues that, for Bultmann, the necessity of an existentialist interpretation follows as a consequence of the fact that we know God as the one who asks questions of our own existence, and little or nothing more.[22] He writes, "Existentialist interpretation . . . also restricts the question about the contemporary significance

18. Dilthey, *Selected Writings*, 226–27.

19. Pannenberg, *BQT*, vol. 1, 105.

20. Pannenberg, *BQT*, vol. 1, 106.

21. Bultmann, "The Problem of Hermeneutics," 241; and Pannenberg, *BQT*, vol. 1, 107.

22. Pannenberg, *BQT*, vol. 1, 108.

of the past to . . . the question of human existence."[23] Bultmann's *theological* basis is inadequate, relying on "human
nature." He shares too much with Dilthey and Heidegger.
Nevertheless, Pannenberg firmly endorses the widespread
recognition of the need for "pre-understanding," and acknowledges that Fuchs and Ebeling went part of the way
in their "New Hermeneutic."[24] At least, like Bultmann, they
regarded the text of the New Testament as making a claim,
calling us, and addressing us.

(ii) Pannenberg and Gadamer

The most recent major exponent of hermeneutics in the
German tradition is Hans-Georg Gadamer. Pannenberg
regards his central theme as that of "language-event"
(*Sprachereignis*), as in Fuchs. He writes, "Gadamer excel-
lently describes the way in which the past and the present are
brought into relation to each other in the process of understanding as a 'fusion of horizons' (*Horizontverschelzung*)."[25]
The purpose of the word "horizon," which Pannenberg
favors, is to acknowledge that the interpreter's horizon is
not fixed, but capable of movement and expansion. Pannenberg writes, "In the process of understanding, the
interpreter's horizon is widened in such a way that the
initially strange matter along with its own horizon can be
appropriated into the *expanded horizon* he attains as he
understands. In the interpreter's encounter with his text, *a
new horizon is formed*."[26]

This fits admirably with Pannenberg's vision that
understanding entails *ever-expanding* horizons *within*

23. Pannenberg, *BQT*, vol. 1, 109.
24. Pannenberg, *BQT*, vol. 1, 113–14.
25. Pannenberg, *BQT*, vol. 1, 117.
26. Pannenberg, *BQT*, vol. 1, also 117 (my italics).

which truth may be perceived. It brings us back to our earlier key theme that since God is the God of all reality, and since we aim at understanding universal history, the wider and more comprehensive our theological horizon of understanding can become, the closer we come to God's revelation in Jesus Christ. Pannenberg quotes Gadamer's words to the effect that the elevation to a higher universality, which overcomes not only one's own particularity, but also that of the other, corresponds to a successful conversation, in which a *transformation occurs* into *mutual* possession of understanding.

Gadamer at this point is speaking of historically-effected consciousness (*Wirkungsgeschichte*) and the essence of hermeneutic experience. Genuine experience, he says, is experience of one's own historicity, or historical finitude. He writes:

> Historical consciousness knows about the otherness of the other. . . . The claims of a text . . . really say something to us. Here is where openness belongs. But ultimately this openness does not exist only for the person who speaks; rather, anyone who listens is fundamentally open. Without such openness to one another there is no genuine human bond. . . . Openness to the other, then, involves recognising that I myself must accept some things that are against me, even though no one else forces me to do so.[27]

Pannenberg adds that while in conversation, the partner takes care to avoid premature absorption into the other's horizon. It is important that a single new horizon is formed in the hermeneutical experience. That is why hermeneutical understanding is "always a creative act."[28]

27. Gadamer, *Truth and Method*, 361.
28. Pannenberg, *BQT*, vol. 1, 119.

In our introduction I mentioned personal recollections of conversations with Wolfhart Pannenberg. One of the most interesting and productive was a conversation about the impact and validity of the claims of Gadamer. Pannenberg observed that there was much wisdom in Gadamer's *Truth and Method*, but that he too easily dismissed the importance of factual propositions.

In *Basic Questions in Theology*, Pannenberg observes, "The primary hermeneutical task consists precisely in restoring the word of a transmitted text to its original, if also unspoken, context of meaning. . . . In the course of the interpretation . . . [it is] turned into something that is asserted."[29] A second point of difference is that Gadamer does not explicitly defend what Pannenberg calls "the comprehensive horizon of history." Pannenberg speaks of "the projection of a total understanding of reality which, in view of the distance between the interpreter and the tradition he is interpreting, can only be a historically differentiated one, . . . a mediation of the present by the totality of history."[30] Nevertheless, he also writes: "Gadamer is right when he observes that genuine experience is that experience in which man becomes aware of his finitude."[31]

In the light of Hegel's philosophy, Pannenberg seeks to preserve the finitude of human experience and the openness of the future with a conception of universal history.[32] Pannenberg concludes:

> It is precisely this understanding of history as something whose totality is given by the fact that its end has become accessible in a provisional and anticipatory way that is to be gathered today

29. Pannenberg, *BQT*, vol. 1, 126.

30. Pannenberg, *BQT*, vol. 1, 120.

31. Pannenberg, *BQT*, vol. 1, 121.

32. Pannenberg, *BQT*, vol. 1, 135.

from the history of Jesus and its relationship to the Israelite-Jewish tradition. Hegel was unable to see this because the eschatological character of the message of Jesus remained hidden to him.[33]

2. KNOWLEDGE AND FAITH

(i) Argumentation, Reason, and the Holy Spirit

Pannenberg relates knowledge, reason, faith, and truth in two essays in *Basic Questions in Theology,* volume 2.[34] He makes it abundantly clear that faith and knowledge are not exclusive alternatives. Paul, he says, speaks of the grounding of faith upon our knowledge (Rom 6:8–9; 2 Cor 4:13). He writes that against the view that faith must remain a risk,

> I have asserted that the essence of faith must come to harm precisely if in the long run rational conviction about its basis fails to appear. Faith then is easily perverted into blind credulity towards the authority-claim of the preached message; into superstition, owing to its seeming contradiction of better judgement. It is precisely for the sake of the purity of faith that the importance of rational knowledge of its basis has to be emphasised.[35]

Pannenberg clearly asserts that an unconvincing message cannot attain the power to convince simply by appealing to the Holy Spirit.[36] He writes, "Argumentation and the operation of the Spirit are not in competition with each

33. Pannenberg, *BQT*, vol. 1, 135.

34. Pannenberg, "Insight and Faith," and "Faith and Reason" in *BQT*, vol. 2, 28–45 and 46–64.

35. Pannenberg, "Insight and Faith," *BQT*, vol. 2, 28.

36. Pannenberg, "Insight and Faith," *BQT*, vol. 2, 34.

other. In trusting the Spirit, Paul in no way spared himself thinking and arguing."[37] It is not the case, Pannenberg suggests, that saving faith is set in absolute opposition to historical knowledge.

On the other hand, Pannenberg insists that mere acknowledgement of the historical is not enough; it has to be grasped *as an event that has a bearing on me.*[38] Believing trust must be distinguished from thoughtlessness and superstition. Pannenberg has grave reservations about the "subjectivation and individualisation of piety, which has threatened the life of our churches."[39] The problem of knowledge, he says, must be understood in relation to the "already" and "not yet" of eschatology. For Christians, he argues, "The perfect unity of faith and reason has been promised for the eschaton only (1 Cor. 13:12–13)."[40]

In his essay on "Faith and Reason," Pannenberg acknowledges that in some statements, Martin Luther appeared to speak of reason as "a monster" or a source of evil, and even described the gospel as "against all reason." However, he says, the same Luther not only esteemed reason as the highest court of appeal in the natural, worldly, realm, but also affirmed the cooperation of reason in the realm of theology, when it was illuminated by faith and the Holy Spirit.[41] Typically Pannenberg insists that in the face of the modern attack upon the meaningfulness of Christian faith, theology cannot retreat to claiming to shelter behind an appeal to authority.[42] He insists, "The task of a rational

---

37. Pannenberg, "Insight and Faith," *BQT*, vol. 2, 35.

38. Pannenberg, "Insight and Faith," *BQT*, vol. 2, 37.

39. Pannenberg, "Insight and Faith," *BQT*, vol. 2, 43.

40. Pannenberg, "Faith and Reason," *BQT*, vol. 2, 47.

41. Pannenberg, "Faith and Reason," *BQT*, vol. 2, 48.

42. Pannenberg, "Faith and Reason," *BQT*, vol. 2, 51.

account of the truth of faith has acquired an ever more acute urgency in the modern period."[43]

(ii) Concepts of Reason, and Historical Reason

Pannenberg also insists that "reason" is by no means a uniformly defined entity. This is one reason why there are debates and controversies about the relationship between faith and reason. For example, the reason of which Luther spoke was the Aristotelian-Thomistic understanding of reason (*ratio*). But there is also historical reason and so-called receiving reason. In relation to Aristotle's notion of reason, in Luther's day, the content of the Christian faith had to be regarded as "supra-rational and supernatural, i.e., situated beyond the natural range of reason."[44]

Aquinas also viewed the relation between faith and reason in this way. Even Kant retained similar reservations about the scope of reason as such. Since Johann Georg Hamann (1730–88), Johann Gottfried Herder (1744–1803), and Friedrich Jacobi (1743–1819), Pannenberg notes, reason (*Vernunft*) of a more receptive nature found support. But "receiving reason," he continues, also depends on the domination of what is present at hand, and is regarded by many as a Platonic insight. The future played little part in Greek thought. "Faith, on the other hand, is directed toward something future, or toward him who promises and guarantees something future (Heb. 11:1)."[45]

Historical reason, more creatively, leads from Kant and Fichte to Hegel. Further, Pannenberg comments, "The investigation of this historical life of reason was the theme

---

43. Pannenberg, "Faith and Reason," *BQT*, vol. 2, 53.
44. Pannenberg, "Faith and Reason," *BQT*, vol. 2, 56.
45. Pannenberg, "Faith and Reason," *BQT*, vol. 2, 58.

of Wilhelm Dilthey."[46] We have twice discussed Pannenberg's relation to Dilthey, once in relation to the future and once in relation to hermeneutics. We have already virtually alluded to a definitive statement from Dilthey, which is as follows: "One would have to wait for the end of the life and, in the hour of death, survey the whole and ascertain the relation between the whole and its parts. One would have to wait for the end of history to have all the material necessary to determine its meaning."[47]

In this respect, F. LeRon Shults seems to be right that Pannenberg links hermeneutics with epistemology, engages in interdisciplinary dialogue, is committed to intersubjective dialogue, and recognizes the provisionality of our historically embedded understandings.[48] Whether Shults is correct to consider Pannenberg's approach as akin to postmodernity and postfoundationalism is a more difficult issue to assess. For better or worse, the foundationalist controversy is far less prominent in Germany and Britain than in America.

In certain respects, Pannenberg prefers Hegel's formulation to that of Dilthey, except in the latter's specific definition of meaning. Further, he insists, against Dilthey, that the anticipation of a final future cannot be limited to the individual human being because he attains his significance only as a member of a whole society, or the whole human race. This was what Heidegger unfortunately bracketed out.[49] He concludes, "Reflection upon the historical nature of reason has led us into the horizon of eschatology."[50]

46. Pannenberg, "Faith and Reason," *BQT*, vol. 2, 61.

47. Dilthey, *Pattern and Meaning in History*, 106; quoted by Pannenberg, "Faith and Reason," *BQT*, vol. 2, 61.

48. Shults, *The Postfoundationalist Task of Theology*, 237 and 239.

49. Pannenberg, "Faith and Reason," *BQT*, vol. 2, 62.

50. Pannenberg, "Faith and Reason," *BQT*, vol. 2, 62.

3. TRUTH

(i) Contingency and Unity: Greek and Hebrew Understandings

Pannenberg's essay, "What Is Truth?" was written in 1961, and appears in *Basic Questions in Theology* vol. 2, pp. 1–27. There he states, "The truth of God must prove itself anew in the future, and that cannot be undertaken by any logos; on the contrary, only trust can anticipate it."[51] Truth, he says, involves the unity of reality, not particular truths of one kind or another.

The Western view of truth, Pannenberg writes, may be traced back to two routes: the Greek and the Israelite. The Hebrew word for truth is *ĕmet*, of which the underlying verb has the meaning of *standing firm, establishing, supporting.*[52] It suggests "the reliability and the unshakable dependability of a thing or word, and thus also the faithfulness of persons."[53] On the other hand, the Greek uses of the word "truth" have little or no relation to history. Truth often meant, originally, to let something be seen as itself; not to conceal something. Plato, Cratylus, Xenophon, and Aristotle all agreed that *alētheuein* (to be truthful) consists in "reporting what was, just as it appeared."[54] In modern times, Heidegger has called attention to the notion of what is non-concealed.

In Hebrew thought the faithfulness of God is a more *dynamic* concept. For example, God is compared to a shield and buckler (Ps 91:4). Proof of divine constancy still remains open to the future. In the Hebrew tradition, truth is a matter of revelation, but "in a contingent manner" (which does not mean "irrational"). Truth is not a matter of logical

51. Pannenberg, "What Is Truth?" *BQT*, vol. 2, 8.
52. Pannenberg, "What Is Truth?" *BQT*, vol. 2, 1.
53. Pannenberg, "What Is Truth?" *BQT*, vol. 2, 3.
54. Plato, *Cratylus*, 383B; Aristotle, *Metaphysics*, 1011B.

necessity. Pannenberg says that all constancy, whether it be the orders of nature or in the life of nations, is embraced by the truth of God and is grounded in it. He asserts, "The truth of the biblical understanding of truth had to prove itself and must still prove itself today."[55] In an important statement that builds on this starting point, and which we have already quoted, Pannenberg asserts, "*The truth of God must prove itself anew in the future.*"[56] The reason for this is that faithfulness or constancy needs a duration of time in order for the concept to become fully meaningful. This constitutes another side to Pannenberg's insistence on the "contingency" of the truth of God.

(ii) Truth and the Future

Pannenberg argues that conceptions of truth in Western philosophy have often been wide of the mark. Nietzsche expressed his skepticism about Western philosophical views of truth when he defined truth in an exaggerated form as "that kind of error without which a certain species of living being cannot exist."[57] Martin Heidegger, Jean-Paul Sartre (1905–80), and Søren Kierkegaard devalued the universal in truth. On the other hand, Pannenberg asserts, "Conviction about the *creative* character of thought underlines the procedure of modern science."[58] He concludes, "To date, Hegel's system should be regarded as the most significant attempt at a solution to this problem [i.e., the problem of human historicity or historical finitude]. . . . Truth is not to be found already existing somewhere as a finished product

55. Pannenberg, "What Is Truth?" *BQT*, vol. 2, 11.

56. Pannenberg, "What Is Truth?" *BQT*, vol. 2, 8.

57. Nietzsche, "The Will to Power," in *Complete Works*, vol. 15, 20; cited in Pannenberg, "What Is Truth?" *BQT*, vol. 2, 13

58. Pannenberg, "What Is Truth?" *BQT*, vol. 2, 15.

but is instead thought of as history, as process: 'The truth is the whole.'"[59] He continues:

> *Hegel's thesis* that the truth of the whole will be visible only at the end of history approximates [to] the biblical understanding of truth in two respects. It does so, firstly, by the fact that the truth as such is understood *not as timelessly un-changeable but as a process* that runs its course and maintains itself through change. Secondly, it does so by asserting that the *unity of the process, which is full of contradictions while it is under way,* will become visible along with the true meaning of every individual moment in it, *only from the standpoint of its end. What a thing is, is first decided by its future, by what becomes of it.*[60]

However, *not everything* in Hegel's thought is correct, for example, the problem of pantheism. Also, the horizon of the future is lost in Hegel's thought. Hegel no longer has an open future. The unity of truth remains only a *goal* to be striven for. The biblical concept of history and eschatology provides a solution. Pannenberg writes, "The answer lies in the proleptic character of the Christ event. . . . The resurrection of Jesus is indeed infallibly the dawning of the end of history for men who—like Jesus himself—lived in the apocalyptic expectation of the end."[61] Neverthe-less, for them, the onset of the end had occurred only in a preliminary way. This event was confirmed in Jesus' claim that the final destiny of humans is decided by their stand in relation to his message.

Pannenberg concludes,

59. Pannenberg, "What Is Truth?" *BQT*, vol. 2, 21.

60. Pannenberg, "What Is Truth?" *BQT*, vol. 2, 22 (my italics).

61. Pannenberg, "What Is Truth?" *BQT*, vol. 2, 24.

> The proleptic [anticipatory] character of the destiny of Jesus is the basis for the openness of the future for us, despite the fact that Jesus is the ultimate revelation of the God of Israel as the God of all men. And, conversely, without this proleptic character, the fate of Jesus would not be the ultimate revelation of the deity of God, since the openness of the future belongs constitutively to our reality—against Hegel.... The unsurpassability of the Christ event is thereby expressed in a manner much sharper than Hegel—despite the best of intentions![62]

Pannenberg adds: "The proleptic revelation of God in Jesus is at the same time the solution of the impasses in the Hegelian concept of truth.... *That it alone founds the unity of truth means, however, the demonstration of the truth of the Christian message itself.*"[63] Pannenberg repeats that the unity of all reality is conceivable only as a history. He asserts, "The unity of truth is possible only if it includes the contingency of events and the openness of the future. *The unity of truth is constituted only by the proleptic* [or anticipatory] *revelation of God in Jesus Christ.*"[64]

As I commented in the Preface, Pannenberg constantly returns to the truth and themes of God, Christ, the Holy Spirit, history, the church, rationality, ontology, resurrection, creation, hermeneutics, eternity, and especially the Holy Trinity and the future. There can be no doubt about his passion for the central truths of the Christian faith, and for their constructive discussion. In his book *An Introduction to Systematic Theology*, Pannenberg makes two crucial points. First, he says, "In theology the concept of God can never be

---

62. Pannenberg, "What Is Truth?" *BQT*, vol. 2, 25.

63. Pannenberg, "What Is Truth?" *BQT*, vol. 2, 26 (his italics).

64. Pannenberg, "What Is Truth?" *BQT*, vol. 2, 27 (my italics).

simply one issue among others. It is the central issue, around which everything else is organized. . . . Without the reality of God, Jesus' teaching would be deprived of its core."[65] His second point concerns truth. Theology constantly requires "an effort at examining its truth claims."[66]

QUESTIONS FOR DISCUSSION

1. Is Pannenberg right to claim that Schleiermacher, Dilthey, Heidegger, and Bultmann, hold over-subjective views of hermeneutics? Are his reservations and also positive views of Gadamer helpful?

2. How helpful is the traditional view of the hermeneutical circle? Is Pannenberg correct in suggest that this is inevitable, given the interpreter's relation to life?

3. Does Pannenberg's use of the word "horizon" make good sense? How far does his notion of extending larger universal horizons serve theology?

4. How important is Pannenberg's rejection of blind credulity assist our understanding of genuine Christian faith?

5. Is Pannenberg's distinction between different types of human reason helpful or otherwise for Christian theology?

65. Pannenberg, *An Introduction to Systematic Theology*, 21.
66. Pannenberg, *An Introduction to Systematic Theology*, 17.

BIBLIOGRAPHY

BOOKS BY PANNENBERG

Pannenberg, Wolfhart. *Anthropology in Theological Perspective.* 1985. Reprint. London: T. & T. Clark, 2004.

———. *The Apostles' Creed in the Light of Today's Questions* London: SCM, 1972.

———. *Basic Questions in Theology.* London: SCM, 1970–73.

———. "Constructive and Critical Functions of Christian Eschatology." *HTR* 77 (1984) 119–39.

———. *Faith and Reality.* London: Search, 1977.

———. "God's Presence in History." *Christian Century*, March 11, 1981, 260–63. Online: http://www.religion-online.org/article/gods-presence-in-history.

———. "Hermeneutics and Universal History." In *History and Hermeneutic*, 124–52. ET. New York: Harper & Row 1967. (Reprinted in Pannenberg, *Basic Questions in Theology*, vol. 1, 96–136. London: SCM, 1970–73.)

———. *An Introduction to Systematic Theology.* Edinburgh: T. & T. Clark, 1991.

———. *Jesus—God and Man.* ET. London: SCM, 1968.

———. "Protestant Piety and Guilt Consciousness." In *Christian Spirituality and Sacramental Community*, 13–30. London: Darton, Longman & Todd, 1984.

———. "The Question of God." In *Basic Questions in Theology*, 201–33. London: SCM, 1970–73.

———. "Redemptive Event and History." In *Essays on Old Testament Interpretation*, edited by Claus Westermann, 314–35. ET. London: SCM, 1963. (In extended form in Pannenberg, *Basic Questions in Theology*, vol. 1, 15–80. London: SCM, 1970.)

———. "The Revelation of God in Jesus of Nazareth." In *New Frontiers in Theology*, vol. 3, *Theology as History*, edited by James Robinson and John Cobb, 101–33. New York: Harper & Row, 1967.

———. *Metaphysics and the Idea of God*. Edinburgh: T. & T. Clark, 1990.

———. *Systematic Theology*. 3 vols. Grand Rapids: Eerdmans, 1991–98.

———. *Theology and the Kingdom of God*. Philadelphia: Westminster Press, 1969.

———. *Theology and the Philosophy of Science*. Philadelphia: Westminster, 1976.

———. *What Is Man? Contemporary Anthropology in Theological Perspective*. Philadelphia: Fortress, 1972.

Pannenberg, Wolfhart, Rolf Rendtorff, Trutz Rendtorff, and Ulrich Wilckens, eds. *Revelation as History*. New York: MacMillan, 1968.

OTHER BOOKS CITED IN THE TEXT

Aquinas, Thomas. *Summa Theologiae*. Latin with English translation. 60 vols. London: Eyre & Spottiswoode, 1963.

Athanasius. *St. Athanasius on the Incarnation*. London: Mowbray, 1944.

Ayer, Alfred J. *Language, Truth, and Logic*. 2nd ed. London: Gollancz, 1956.

Barth, Karl. *Church Dogmatics*. 14 vols. ET. Edinburgh: T. & T. Clark, 1957–75.

———. *The Epistle to the Romans*. ET. Oxford: Oxford University Press, 1933.

———. "The Strange New World within the Bible." In *The Word of God and the Word of Man*, 28–50. London: Hodder & Stoughton, 1928.

———. *The Word of God and the Word of Man.* London: Hodder & Stoughton, 1928.

Becker, J. Christiaan. *Paul the Apostle.* Edinburgh: T. & T. Clark, 1980.

———. *Paul's Apocalyptic Gospel: The Coming Triumph of God.* Philadelphia: Fortress, 1982.

Bradshaw, Timothy. *Pannenberg: A Guide for the Perplexed.* London: T. & T. Clark, 2009.

Brown, Alexandra. *The Cross in Human Transformation: Paul's Apocalyptic Word in 1 Corinthians.* Minneapolis: Fortress, 1989.

Bultmann, Rudolf. *Essays Philosophical and Theological.* London: SCM, 1955.

———. "The Problem of Hermeneutics." In *Essays Philosophical and Theological*, 234–61. London: SCM Press, 1955.

Calvin, John. *Institutes of the Christian Religion.* 2 vols. London: Clarke, 1957.

Clarke, Samuel. *A Discourse concerning Natural Religion.* 1705. At Eighteenth-century Collections Online: find.galegroup.com.

Clines, David J. A. "The Image of God." *Tyndale Bulletin* 19 (1968) 53–103.

Crombie, Ian M. "Theology and Falsification." In *New Essays in Philosophical Theology*, edited by Antony Flew and Alasdair MacIntyre, 109–30. London: SCM, 1957.

Cullmann, Oscar. *Christ and Time: The Primitive Conception of Time and History.* ET. London: SCM, 1951.

Cyril of Jerusalem. *Catechetical Lectures.* ET. *NPNF*, series 2, vol. 7.

Descartes, René. *Meditations.* ET. Cambridge: Cambridge University Press, 1905.

Dilthey, Wilhelm. *Gesammelte Schriften.* Leipzig: Teubner, 1927.

———. *Pattern and Meaning in History.* Edited by H. P. Rickman. London: Allen & Unwin, 1961.

———. *Selected Writings.* Edited by H. P. Rickman. Cambridge: Cambridge University Press, 1976.

Downing, Gerald. *Has Christianity a Revelation?* London: SCM, 1964.

Ebeling, Gerhard. "Theological Reflections on Conscience." In *Word and Faith*, 407–23. London: SCM, 1963.

Feuerbach, Ludwig. *The Essence of Christianity.* 2nd ed. London: Trübner, 1881.

Fison, J. E. *The Blessing of the Holy Spirit.* New York: Longman's, Green, 1950.

Flew, Antony, ed. *Essays in Philosophical Theology.* London: SCM, 1955.

Bibliography

Gadamer, Hans-Georg. *Truth and Method.* 2nd English ed. London: Sheed & Ward, 1989.

―――. *Warheit und Methode.* Tubingen: Mohr Siebeck, 1960.

Galloway, Allan D. *Wolfhart Pannenberg.* London: Allen & Unwin, 1973.

Gilbertson, Michael. *God and History in the Book of Revelation: New Testament Studies in Dialogue with Pannenberg and Moltmann.* SNTSM, 124. Cambridge: Cambridge University Press, 2003.

Gollwitzer, Helmut. *The Existence of God as Confessed by Faith.* London: SCM, 1965.

Grenz, Stanley. *Reason for Hope: The Systematic Theology of Wolfhart Pannenberg.* New York: Oxford University Press, 1990.

Hamilton, Neill Q. *The Holy Spirit and Eschatology in Paul.* SJT Occasional Papers 6. Edinburgh: Oliver and Boyd 1957.

Hegel, Georg Wilhelm Friedrich. *Lectures on the Philosophy of Religion.* London: Humanities, 1962.

Heidegger, Martin. *Being and Time.* ET. Oxford: Blackwell, 1962.

Hick, John. *Philosophy of Religion.* Englewood Cliffs, NJ: Prentice-Hall, 1963.

Hume, David. *A Treatise of Human Nature.* 1739. Reprint. Oxford: Oxford University Press, 1978.

Jones, O. R. *The Concept of Holiness.* London: Allen & Unwin, 1961.

Kant, Immanuel. *Critique of Pure Reason.* 1781. ET. London: Bell, 1905.

Koch, Klaus. *The Rediscovery of Apocalyptic.* London: SCM, 1972.

Kuhn, Thomas S. *The Structure of Scientific Revolutions.* 2nd ed. Chicago: Chicago University Press, 1970. (1st ed., 1962.)

Küng, Hans. *Does God Exist?* London: Collins, 1978.

―――. *Freud and the Problem of God.* New Haven, CT: Yale University Press, 1990.

Käsemann, Ernst. *New Testament Questions of Today.* London: SCM, 1969.

Leibniz Gottfried W. *Discourse in Metaphysics and the Monadology.* Chicago: Open Court, 1902.

Lossky, Vladimir. *The Mystical Theology of the Eastern Church.* New York: St Vladimir's Seminary Press, 1976.

McLean, John. *From the Future: Getting to Grips with Pannenberg's Thought.* Milton Keynes: Paternoster, 2013.

Migliore, Daniel L. *Faith Seeking Understanding: An Introduction to Christian Theology.* Grand Rapids: Eerdmans, 1991.

Moltmann, Jürgen. *The Coming of God: Christian Eschatology.* ET. London: SCM, 1996.

————. *God in Creation: An Ecological Doctrine of Creation.* ET. London: SCM, 1985.

————. *The Spirit of Life: A Universal Affirmation.* ET. London: SCM, 1992.

————. *The Trinity and the Kingdom of God: The Doctrine of God.* ET. London: SCM, 1981.

Mostert, Christiaan. *God and the Future: Wolfhart Pannenberg's Eschatological Doctrine of God.* London: T. & T. Clark, 2002.

Neuhaus, Richard J. "Wolfhart Pannenberg: Profile of a Theologian." In Pannenberg, *Theology and the Kingdom of God,* 9–50. Philadelphia: Westminster, 1969.

Niebuhr, Reinhold. *The Nature and Destiny of Man: A Christian Interpretation.* 2 vols. London: Nisbet, 1941.

Nietzsche, Friedrich. *The Complete Works.* 18 vols. Reprint. London: Read Books, 2013.

————. *The Twilight of the Idols and the Anti-Christ.* London: Penguin, 1968.

Osborne, Grant R. *The Hermeneutical Spiral.* Downers Grove, IL: InterVarsity, 1991.

Otto, Rudolf. *The Idea of the Holy.* ET. London: Oxford University Press, 1923.

Paton, H. J. *The Modern Predicament: A Study in the Philosophy of Religion.* London: Allen and Unwin, 1955.

Plantinga, Alvin. *God and Other Minds.* Ithaca, NY: Cornell University Press, 1967.

————. *God, Freedom, and Evil.* New York: Harper and Row, 1974.

————. *The Nature of Necessity.* Oxford: Oxford University Press, 1974.

Popper Karl. *The Logic of Scientific Discovery.* London: Hutcheson, 1959.

Price, H. H. *Belief.* London: Allen and Unwin, 1969.

Ramsey, Ian T. *Religious Language: An Empirical Placing of Theological Phrases.* London: SCM, 1957.

Robinson, J. A. T. *Honest to God.* London: SCM, 1963.

Rogers, Eugene. *After the Spirit: A Constructive Pneumatology from Resources Outside the Modern West.* London: SCM, 2006.

Schleiermacher, Friedrich D. E. *Hermeneutics: The Handwritten Manuscripts.* Missoula, MT: Scholars, 1977.

Schlink, Edmund. *The Coming Christ and the Coming Church.* Edinburgh: Oliver & Boyd, 1967.

Schnackenburg, Rudolf. *Baptism in the Thought of Paul.* Oxford: Blackwell, 1964.

Shults, F. LeRon. *The Postfoundationalist Task of Theology: Wolfhart Pannenberg and the New Theological Rationality*. Grand Rapids: Eerdmans, 1999.

Stendahl, Krister. "The Apostle Paul and the Introspective Conscience of the West." In *Paul among Jews and Gentiles*, 78–96. London: SCM, 1977.

Thiselton, Anthony C. *Approaching the Study of Theology*. London: SPCK, 2017.

———. *Doubt, Faith and Certainty*. Grand Rapids: Eerdmans, 2017.

———. *The First Epistle to the Corinthians: A Commentary on the Greek Text*. NIGTC. Grand Rapids: Eerdmans, 2000.

———. *The Holy Spirit: In Biblical Teaching, through the Centuries, and Today*. Grand Rapids: Eerdmans, 2013.

———. *Life after Death*. Grand Rapids: Eerdmans, 2012.

———. *New Horizons in Hermeneutics*. London: Harper Collins, 1992.

———. *A Shorter Guide to the Holy Spirit: Bible, Doctrine, Experience*. Grand Rapids: Eerdmans, 2016.

———. *Systematic Theology*. Grand Rapids: Eerdmans, 2015.

———. *The Thiselton Companion to Christian Theology*. Grand Rapids: Eerdmans, 2015.

———. *The Two Horizons: New Testament Hermeneutics and Philosophical Description*. Exeter, UK: Paternoster, 1980.

Torrance, Thomas F. *Theological Science*. London: Oxford University Press, 1969.

Tupper, E. Frank. *The Theology of Wolfhart Pannenberg*. London: SCM, 1974.

Watson, John B. *Behaviorism*. 1913. Reprint. New York: Norton, 1970.

Wenz, Gunther. *Introduction to Wolfhart Pannenberg's Systematic Theology*. Gottingen: Vandenhoeck & Ruprecht, 2013.

Wisdom, John. "Gods." 1944–45. In *Logic and Language*, edited by Antony Flew, 187–205. Oxford: Blackwell, 1955.

Wittgenstein, Ludwig. *Philosophical Investigations*. Oxford: Blackwell, 1958.

———. *Zettel*. Oxford: Blackwell, 1967.

INDEX OF NAMES

INDEX OF SUBJECTS

SCRIPTURE INDEX

NEW TESTAMENT

Made in the USA
Monee, IL
28 August 2021